CLINTON
—ON—
CLINTON

CLINTON
ON
CLINTON

A PORTRAIT *of the* PRESIDENT
IN HIS OWN WORDS

EDITED BY WAYNE MEYER

Perennial
An Imprint of HarperCollinsPublishers

This book is published by arrangement with Bill Adler Books, Inc.

CLINTON ON CLINTON. Copyright © 1999 by Bill Adler Books, Inc. All rights reserved. Printed in the United States of America. No part of this book may be used or reproduced in any manner whatsoever without written permission except in the case of brief quotations embodied in critical articles and reviews. For information address HarperCollins Publishers Inc., 10 East 53rd Street, New York, NY 10022.

HarperCollins books may be purchased for educational, business, or sales promotional use. For information please write: Special Markets Department, HarperCollins Publishers Inc., 10 East 53rd Street, New York, NY 10022.

First Avon edition published 1999.

Reprinted in Perennial 2004.

Library of Congress Cataloging-in-Publication Data

Clinton, Bill.
    Clinton on Clinton : a portrait of the president in his own words / edited by Wayne Meyer.
        p. cm.
    1. Clinton, Bill, 1946– Quotations. 2. Presidents—United States—Quotations. 3. United States—Politics and government—1993—Quotations, maxims, etc. I. Meyer, Wayne. II. Title.
    E838.5.C552   1999   99-33499
    973.929'092—dc21   CIP

ISBN 0-380-80279-1

04 05 06 07 08 JTC/RRD 10 9 8 7 6 5 4 3 2 1

I am most grateful to Virginia Fay for her creative efforts in helping me put this book together.

Contents

CLINTON
—ON—
CLINTON

Early Life

CHILDHOOD

William Jefferson Blythe IV was born on August 19, 1946.

———

"Fifty years ago, when I was born in a summer storm to a widowed mother in a little town in Arkansas, it was unthinkable that I might have ever become president."

———

"There are positive and negative things coming out of my childhood. If you had clothes on your back and a place to sleep and food to eat and you had people to love you and to discipline you, you were by definition not poor; you were rich, because you had the elements of a successful life. There was no sense of entitlement to anything more."

———

"I think my desire to accommodate is probably due in part to the sense that I had from my childhood, that I was the person who had to hold things together in my home, to keep peace. And on balance, those skills are very good . . . I mean, basically, we're living in a world where cooperation is better than conflict."

———

"My mother and my family gave me this sense of resilience and just enjoying life. Most of the people in my grandfather's generation, whom I knew very well—my great-aunts and my uncles and all that—they all had a kind of happy-go-lucky, upbeat outlook on life. Most of the family were living in quite modest circumstances, had grown up in the Depression or before. Never had much of

2

anything. They had the idea that nobody owes you anything, you're not entitled to anything good, you gotta take what comes, and you just can't give up. Quitting is a form of cowardice, and you just can't do it."

Grandparents/Great-Grandparents

"I lived with my grandparents* until I was four, and they had a lot to do with my early commitment to learning. They taught me to count and read—I was reading little books when I was three. They didn't have much formal education, but they helped imbed in me a real sense of educational achievement that was reinforced at home."

"My grandfather had almost no education but was an instinctive liberal on race. He owned a little grocery store in Hope, Arkansas. More than half his customers were black. And if he knew them, and he knew they were doing the best they could, he would give them food even if they didn't have money. My grandfather supported integration and thought black people were getting a raw deal. In a little Southern town, you actually know black people, so people who were not blinded by racism had the advantage of human contact."

"My grandfather was the kindest person I ever knew. Yet my grandfather's personality trait was a fault because it was to prove ruinous to him in business."

*His maternal grandparents, Edith Valeria Grisham Cassidy and James Eldridge Cassidy.

3

After freshman year at Georgetown, his (step) grandfather Allen W.
Clinton took ill. He wrote to friend Denise Hyland:

"My grandfather is dying tonight, Denise. Mother and Daddy just left, all the family is beginning to congregate. He is a fine old gentleman of eighty-five and until two years ago he produced some of the best vegetables you ever saw in his acre garden. Worked at the garage until the very end. He was never much of a churchgoer, but I have a hunch he is going to have a good trip."

———

His Mother, Virginia Dell Cassidy Blythe Clinton Dwire Kelley

His mother left him with her parents while she trained to become a
nurse-anesthetist. He later described her departure at the train station:

"I remember my mother crying and actually falling down on her knees by the railbed. And my grandmother saying, 'She's doing this for you.' "

———

"She was, I thought, a good role model in three ways. She always worked; did a good job as a parent; and we had a lot of adversity in our life when I was growing up, and she handled it real well, and I think she gave me a high pain threshold, which, I think, is a very important thing to have in public life. You have to be able to take a lot of criticism—suffer defeats and get up tomorrow and fight again."

———

Asked what made her a great mother:

"First of all, her incredible resilience. She was always encouraging me to try new things, to keep going, to never be deterred by defeat. But I think it's important to point out that I never felt that I was under some burden to achieve. She made our life fun even in the difficult times."

———

On State Department personnel searching his and his mother's passport files during the 1992 campaign:

"Now it turns out that the State Department was not only rifling through my files, but was actually investigating my mother—a well-known subversive. It would be funny if it were not so pathetic. This is a crowd so desperate to win that they have forgotten the purpose of power in a democratic government is to help people and to lift them up."

———

"I'm not worried about her because my mother has dealt with people a lot tougher than George Bush."

———

From acceptance speech, July 16, 1992:

"My mother taught me. She taught me about family and hard work and sacrifice. She held steady through tragedy after tragedy. And she held our family, my brother and I, together through tough times. As a child, I watched her go off to work each day at a time when it wasn't always easy to be a working mother.

"As an adult, I've watched her fight off breast cancer. And again she has taught me a lesson in courage. And always, always she taught me to fight."

———

Women's Leadership Forum, July 17, 1996:

"You know, my mother, bless her soul, had a lot of interesting qualities—but one of the things I learned from her at an early age is that she never begrudged another soul their success. She never did. If somebody else was doing well, it made her happy. Even if they didn't like her, it made her happy. It didn't bother her, ever. All she ever wanted to do was to get a fair deal and have a chance to be happy, too.''

Democratic National Convention, Chicago, Illinois, August 29, 1996:

''Everywhere I've gone in America, people come up and talk to me about their struggle with the demands of work and their desire to do a better job with their children. The very first person I ever saw fight that battle was here with me four years ago, and tonight I miss her very, very much. My irrepressible, hardworking, always optimistic mother did the best she could for her, (my) brother and me, often against very stiff odds. I learned from her just how much love and determination can overcome.

''But from her and from our life, I also learned that no parent can do it alone. And no parent should have to. She had the kind of help every parent deserves—from our neighbors, our friends, our teachers, our pastors, our doctors, and so many more.''

On his mother's death on January 6, 1994:

''I went into the kitchen and got halfway to the phone before I realized that I couldn't call her . . . A lot of people who lose a mother or father or husband or wife will tell you that, they find themselves almost talking out loud. I do that a lot.''

On a visit to Prague in April 1994, he visited bars with Vaclav Havel as diplomacy dictated. The Czechs discreetly asked if he felt comfortable with the festivities in view of his mother's recent death:

''My mother would have wondered why I hadn't drunk more beer on this trip.''

"As a child, I saw her go off to work each day in an era when it wasn't easy to be a working mother. As an adult, I marveled as she threw herself into politics to help me through victory and defeat, and encouraged my brother in his career while never giving up her unshakable belief that he could recover from his drug problem. And I watched with admiration as she endured his own disappointments with good humor and determination, always enjoying life and living it to the fullest, even as she battled the breast cancer that finally took her from us when she was seventy years old."

His Father, William Jefferson Blythe III

"The most profound event was something that occurred before I was born, which is the death of my father. It's a very difficult thing to be raised with a myth in a lot of ways. All of my relatives attempted to make it a positive rather than a negative thing, but I think I always felt in some sense that I needed to hurry because my father's death gave me a real sense of mortality. I mean, most kids never think about when they're going to run out of time, when they might die. I thought about it all the time because my father died at twenty-nine. By the same token, now I feel as if I've had a very full life. I mean whatever happens to me, I've already outlived him by fifteen years. So I've always had a different view than most people have. Being in such a hurry to accomplish things is both good and bad. Having my own child was probably one of the things that enabled me to get off that kind of career track. It was one of the reasons in 1987 that I decided not to run for president. Just being able to have a family life mattered to me and having that whole set of experiences that I didn't even imagine when I was a child growing up had a big impact on me."

"I guess in ways I never permitted myself to admit, I missed my father terribly. I think because my father had died and my mother was probably a little too protective, I always had a desire to avoid conflict, which has led my political enemies to underestimate me."

"But, anyway, I think when I was younger, that's one of the reasons I was always in a hurry. And I also think I thought I had to live for myself and for him, too. I sort of had to meet a very high standard of conduct and accomplishment, in part because of his absence. It's a funny thing, but the older I get the more I realize that sort of shaped my childhood—that great memory."

"My psychological clock was tuned to the idea that you might only get to live twenty-nine years, and that made me much more driven to do everything I could in life as soon as I could."

His Stepfather, Roger Clinton, Sr.

When he was four, his mother married Roger Clinton:

"He was a wonderful person, but he didn't like himself very much. He had a prolonged bout with cancer. And I think in the course of fighting it through somehow, he gained some peace with himself that enabled him to reconcile with all the rest of us. He was a marvelous person, and he was very good to me. It really was a painful experience to see someone you love, that you think a lot of, that you care about, just in the grip of a demon."

"I loved having a father. I loved having a man around the house that I could just be with, and it pained me to see him as withdrawn as he became, just unable to get outside of himself anymore."

———

"I remember the police coming and taking him away. That was a pretty spooky deal . . . I remember it like it was yesterday."

———

On the now famous incident when fourteen-year-old Bill Clinton broke in the door and stopped his stepfather beating his mother:

"I just broke down the door of their room one night when they were having an encounter and told him that I was bigger than him now, and there would never be any more of this while I was there."

———

He separated his mother and brother from his stepfather:

"You will never hit either of them again. If you want them, you'll have to go through me."

———

"That was a dramatic thing. It made me know I could do it if I had to. But it made me more conflict-averse. It's a really painful thing, you know, to threaten to beat up your stepfather."

———

After the divorce, he took his stepfather's surname legally at age fifteen:

"I decided it was something I ought to do. I thought it would be a gesture of family solidarity. And I thought it would be good for my brother, who was coming up."

———

"A man's name doesn't make any difference in the world, Mother. It's the man."

———

While at Georgetown, he visited his stepfather at Duke University Hospital during his final illness. He wrote to his mother:

"Daddy seems better but so very anxious to get home. He is mentally and physically more alert than I have seen him since he started having eye trouble. Of course, the treatments take away his appetite and make him sick, but that goes with it . . .

"Hope you will have some time to yourself other than the races now—probably you will never win that much. What a girl!—I know how hard this has been for you—my goodness, your life has been a succession of crises, all of which you've weathered.

"Surely I am prouder of you than you could ever be of me. . . ."

———

Another letter during this period:

"I never will forget it. We went to Easter service at the Duke chapel, and then I drove him slowly around the Triangle there. After that, we went over to Chapel Hill and saw all the dogwoods, the redbud trees. It was just stunningly beautiful. It was one of the most beautiful days I can ever remember in my entire life. And it was a wonderful experience we had, just the two of us."

———

George J. "Jeff" Dwire

After the death of Roger Clinton, his mother married Jeff Dwire, a hairdresser, in 1968. In 1956, Dwire had been convicted in a stock-fraud case and had spent time in prison. Years later, he sought a pardon.

From a letter on behalf of Jeff Dwire's pardon request:

"Besides that relationship there is our close friendship. When I am able to go home, we talk for hours on end, and I am continually amazed at the breadth of his knowledge, especially in the fields of my primary interest, politics and law. Few citizens are more conscientious students of public affairs; few have a better grasp of the great issues that face the nation today. If ever a man deserved to have his vote returned to him, this one does. There are, then, the following statements I can make without reservation about Jeff Dwire. He has worked hard and been successful. He has overcome the initial reservations many people had about him and is much respected by the members of our community, including the chief of police. And he has made a family life that is a truly wonderful thing to observe and to be a part of. I have known great and famous men who have not done better. I doubt very much that I will be able to do better. If Jeff Dwire is not worthy of pardon, then I do not see how any of the rest of us are worthy to be citizens."

———

Jeff Dwire died in 1974 after complications from diabetes.

———

From his eulogy for Jeff Dwire:

"Jeff Dwire was an extremely personal man, and so we thought it appropriate that someone who knew and loved him personally, intimately, should offer a few remembrances of him. Many will recall how debonair, sometimes even flamboyant, he was in his wonderfully bright-colored clothes. Others will remember how he

11

loved to go places and party and enjoy life with his family and friends. Still others will note that he was one of the most intelligent, versatile men—one of those who seemed to know something about everything—that they ever knew. But what was really important about his life is that he worked so hard at it and that his real joy came from giving to others. You can see it in the little children whose lives he touched with so much tenderness. You can see it in the old, the poor, the unschooled to whom he gave work and whom he treated with such dignity. You can see it in those who worked for him and those who called him friend, in their grief at losing a man whose like they will not see again."

———

His mother later married retired food broker Richard Kelley in 1982.

———

Family Life

"My brother and I were sort of two prototypical kids of an alcoholic family."

———

When asked if that meant they had only two options, become a president or a coke dealer, he answered:

"Well, a lot of the literature suggests that's exactly what happens to children of alcoholics.

"Sometimes they do both in different ways . . . I understand addictive behavior. You know, a compulsive politician is probably not far from that."

———

On his family's troubled history:

"I was forty years old by the time I was sixteen."

_____

His Brother, Roger Clinton, Jr.

Roger Clinton, Junior, was born in 1956.

_____

In 1984, during Clinton's fourth race for governor, he learned that his brother was involved in drug trafficking. Clinton was told about it about a month before Roger was arrested and had to keep the secret:

"I couldn't tell my mother; or her husband, or my brother. It was a nightmare. But it was the right thing to do. He had a four-gram-a-day habit. They said if he hadn't been in incredible physical shape, he would have died."

_____

On his brother Roger's drug addition and conviction for dealing cocaine:

"I never knew whether my brother or my mother would forgive me, but I had to be governor, not brother, not son."

_____

The governor issued a statement:

"This is a time of great pain and sadness for me and my family. My brother has apparently become involved with drugs, a curse which has reached epidemic proportions and has plagued the lives of millions of families in our nation, including many in our state. I ask for the prayers of our people at this difficult time for my brother, for my family, and for me. I love my brother very much and will try to be of comfort to him, but I want his case to be handled as any other similar case would be. Because this matter is now in court, I will have no further comment."

———

Roger was sentenced to two years and served a little over a year in federal prison.

———

School Days

"The teachers whom I really liked were, first of all, demanding. They made us work hard, and they gave hard tests. I tended to do better, by the way, all my life in the hard courses than the easy courses."

———

As a fifth grader, he was already attracted to politics, and avidly followed the 1956 campaign:

"I was hooked on politics then and there. It got to me in a way on television that no amount of reading in the newspapers about candidates running for office and politics in general could impact me."

———

On the 1960 campaign:

"I was gung ho for politics by then. My teacher in ninth-grade civics class was Mary Marty, and she had the class debating the merits of the two candidates for the White House.

"Mrs. Marty and I were the only ones in the class who were for the JFK-LBJ ticket. Since Hot Springs is the seat of government

14

for Garland County and is heavily Republican, my teacher and I were like outcasts in an environment that had everyone else rooting for Nixon and Lodge. But when that Wednesday morning rolled around after the Tuesday of November 8, Mrs. Marty and I were the jubilant ones in the classroom.

"I was at the TV set all night, hoping and praying for Kennedy's victory. What a rewarding moment it was for me when Nixon made his concession speech."

———

Music

"All my musical competitions were great because it was so competitive, but, in a way, you were fighting against yourself. And music, to me, was—is—kind of representative of everything I like most in life. It's beautiful and fun but very rigorous. If you wanted to be good, you had to work like crazy. And it was a real relationship between effort and reward. My musical life experiences were just as important to me, in terms of forming my development, as my political experiences or my academic life."

———

"I used to play my saxophone a lot, sometimes when I was angry but usually when I was lonely. I could play for hours and hours and hours, and I wouldn't be lonely anymore."

———

At a fund-raiser early in the 1992 campaign, he played his saxophone with the band:

"The secret is always to play with a good, loud band."

———

15

Boys' Nation

At age seventeen he attended Boys' State, a camp where kids learned about politics. He was elected a delegate to Boys' Nation and won a trip to Washington, D.C., in 1963.

———

In Washington with Boys' Nation he met Senator J. William Fulbright and President John F. Kennedy:

"I decided to be a Democrat, starting in the presidential election of 1960, when John Kennedy excited me with a promise to get the country moving again. I think he gave people the sense that they could make a difference. And he did it without ever promising that all the problems could be solved—just that tomorrow would be better than today. He convinced me that he and Lyndon Johnson wanted to do something about civil-rights problems, particularly in the South, my own region."

———

"When I came up here to Boys' Nation and we had this mock congressional session I was one of only three or four Southerners who would even vote for the civil-rights plank. That's largely because of my family. My grandfather had a grade-school education and ran a grocery store across the street from the cemetery in Hope, Arkansas, where my parents and my grandparents are buried. Most of his customers were black, were poor, and were working people. As a child in that store I saw that people of different races could treat each other with respect and dignity.

"But I also saw that the black neighborhood across the street was the only one in town where the streets weren't paved. And when I returned to that neighborhood in the late sixties to see a woman who had cared for me as a toddler, the streets still weren't paved."

16

Georgetown

He chose to attend Georgetown because it was in Washington, D.C.

"By the time I was seventeen, I knew I wanted to be [a politician] . . . and I knew that if I was in school in Washington I would have many opportunities to learn a lot about foreign affairs, domestic politics, and economics . . . I just started asking people, including staff members of our congressional delegation, what was the most appropriate place. The consensus was that the School of Foreign Service at Georgetown was the most appropriate and the most academically respected and rigorous."

"I knew that politically, it would be advantageous for me to stay here [Arkansas] to go to school, but I felt that if I went away to school and exposed myself to the rest of the country and learned something about the rest of the world, then if I ever could get elected down here, I'd do a better job."

Leaving Georgetown with His Mother after Orientation:

"Don't worry, Mother. By the time I leave here they'll know why they let me in."

Clinton enrolled in Georgetown in 1964. Because he had to work to pay his way, he applied to work for Senator William Fulbright.

Fulbright's administrative assistant Lee Williams, called him in Hot Springs.

"He said, 'Well, you can have a part-time job for $3,500 a year or a full-time job for $5,000.' And I said 'How about two part-time jobs?' And this is a verbatim conversation—he said, 'You're just the guy I'm looking for.' He said, 'Be here Monday.' And that's a true story. It was Friday morning. I'd had no sleep. I got up, got all my bags packed and everything, and I was there Monday for work."

"As a teenager, I heard John Kennedy's summons to citizenship. And then, as a student at Georgetown, I heard that call clarified by a professor . . . Carroll Quigley, who said America was the greatest country in the history of the world because our people have always believed in two great ideas: first, that tomorrow can be better than today, and second, that each of us has a personal, moral responsibility to make it so."

Address before the Diplomatic Corps, Georgetown University, Washington, D.C., January 18, 1993:

"I came to this university at a time when a fallen president had asked my generation to give something back to our country. I was looking for a place to prepare for that calling. Georgetown and its School of Foreign Service have made enormous contributions not only to my life but to public service in general."

At Georgetown he took a religion class for non-Catholics taught by the dean of the School of Foreign Service, Father Joseph Sebes.

———

"We went through all these cultures and all their religions and no matter how different they were, it was obvious they all had a hunger to find some meaning in their lives beyond the temporal things that consume most of us through most of our days. I really developed an immense appreciation for that."

———

From a 1992 speech at Notre Dame, referring to his years at Georgetown University:

"I love the Catholic understanding of history and tradition and how they shape us."

———

Oxford

He applied for and won a Rhodes scholarship.

———

Oxford, 1968:

"The first two weeks I was there I bet I walked fourteen hours a day. I visited all the colleges, went in all the churches, walked through all the parks."

———

On his years at Oxford:

"Being in England was incredible. I got to travel a lot. I got to spend a lot of personal time—learn things, go see things. I read about three hundred books both years I was there."

The Draft

From a letter to Colonel Eugene Holmes, Director of the ROTC at the University of Arkansas, December 3, 1969:

"I have written and spoken and marched against the war. One of the national organizers of the Vietnam Moratorium is a close friend of mine. After I left Arkansas last summer, I went to Washington to work in the national headquarters of the Moratorium, then to England to organize the Americans here for demonstrations October 15 and November 16."

"I didn't see, in the end, how my going in the army and maybe going to Vietnam would achieve anything except a feeling that I had punished myself and gotten what I deserved."

He wrote to Colonel Holmes after winning a high lottery number in the draft:

"First I want to thank you, not just for saving me from the draft, but for being so kind and decent to me last summer, when I was as low as I have ever been. One thing which made the bond we struck in good faith somewhat palatable to me was my high regard for you personally. In retrospect, it seems that the admiration might not have been mutual had you known a little more about me, about my political beliefs and activities. At least you might have thought me more fit for the draft than for the ROTC.

"The decision not to register and related subsequent decisions were the most difficult of my life. I decided to accept the draft in spite of my beliefs for one reason: to maintain my political viability within the system. For years I have worked to prepare myself for a political life characterized by both practical political ability and concern for rapid social progress. It is a life I still feel compelled to try to lead. I do not think our system of government is by definition corrupt, however dangerous and inadequate it has been in recent years. The society may be corrupt, but that is not the same thing, and if that is true we are all finished anyway."

———

"I was a World War II kid. I grew up on John Wayne movies, and I was having all these terrible conflicts over the war."

———

On his antiwar activities during Vietnam:

"I have nothing to hide concerning my antiwar experience. My opposition to the war was well known.

"I've never hidden what I felt about it or what I did. I think I was right . . . I attended two antiwar rallies, one in Washington and one in London."

———

Marijuana

"When I was twenty-two years old in England and I thought there were no consequences, I tried marijuana a couple of times.

"If I had known then what I know now, I would not have done it."

21

During the 1992 campaign:

"I've never broken a state law, but when I was in England I experimented with marijuana a time or two, and I didn't like it. I didn't inhale it, and never tried it again."

———

When asked why he had never disclosed this before:

"Nobody's ever asked me that question point-blank."

———

On telling Chelsea about his marijuana use:

"I think this business about how baby boomers all feel too guilt-ridden to talk to their children is the biggest load of hooey I ever heard. They have a bigger responsibility to talk to their children."

———

"It hadn't bothered me to tell her that she shouldn't make the same mistakes I did."

———

Yale Law School

"The biggest thing that happened to me at law school was meeting Hillary."

———

MEETING HILLARY RODHAM

To friend Carolyn Yeldell during Georgetown years:

"The woman I marry is going to be very independent. She's going to work outside the house. She needs to have her own interest and her own life and not be wrapped up entirely in my life."

———

"It was sort of a fluky deal how it happened. I'd just broken up with another girl, and the last thing I wanted was to get involved with anybody. We were in a class together where—I'm embarrassed to say this, I don't want to set a bad example—neither one of us attended this particular class very often because the guy who taught the class had written the textbook and it was one of those deals where the book was better than the movie. He was a great writer—not a particularly great lecturer, you know.

"But, anyway, I saw her there one day and I followed her out and I didn't have enough courage to talk to her. The truth is I followed her out of the class. So a couple of days later she saw me in the library, and this guy was trying to talk me into joining the Yale Law Review and telling me I could clerk for the U.S. Supreme Court if I were a member of the Yale Law Review and then I could go to New York and make a ton of money and all that kind of stuff.

"And I kept telling him I didn't want to do all of that. I wanted to go home to Arkansas. It didn't matter to anybody whether I was on the Yale Law Review or not. And they were trying to get Southerners, they wanted geographical balance on the Law Review . . . I just didn't much want to do it. And all this time I was talking to this guy about the Law Review, I was looking at Hillary at the other end of the library. And the Yale Law School Library is a real long, narrow [room]. She was down at the other end, and . . . I just was staring at her . . . And she closed this book, and she walked all the way down the library . . . and she

23

came up to me and she said, 'Look, if you're going to keep staring at me, and I'm going to keep staring back, I think we should at least know each other: I'm Hillary Rodham. What's your name?' "

———

Clinton couldn't remember his name.

———

"I was so embarrassed. But that's a true story. That's exactly how we met. It turned out she knew who I was. But I didn't know that at the time either. But I was real impressed that she did that. And we've been together, more or less, ever since."

———

On his first impression of Hillary:
"I could just look at her and tell she was interesting and deep."

———

"I just liked—I liked being around her, because I thought I'd never be bored being with her. In the beginning, I used to tell her that I would like being old with her. That I thought that was an important thing—to be with someone you thought you'd always love being old with."

———

"I remember being genuinely afraid of falling in love with her. She was a star."

Quoted in Vanity Fair:

"I loved being with her, but I had very ambivalent feelings about getting involved with her."

——

University of Arkansas Law School

He told Hillary:

"All I want to be is a country lawyer. I'm going back to Arkansas to become just that."

——

After leaving Yale, Professor Marvin Chirelstein suggested he apply to the University of Arkansas Law School in Fayetteville because it had two vacancies. Reaching Arkansas, Clinton called Wylie Davis, Dean of the Law School:

"I don't have anything set to do, but I'm coming home to Arkansas, and you might want me to come teach up there a year because I'll teach anything, and I don't mind working, and I don't believe in tenure, so you can get rid of me any time you want."

——

Told that at age twenty-six he was too young when applying to teach at the University of Arkansas Law School:

"That's the story of my life. I've always been told that I'm too young for everything I've ever done."

——

He got the job.

Later Hillary Rodham took the other opening and taught there as well.

MARRIAGE

He first asked Hillary to marry him in 1974:

"I know this is a really hard choice for you because I'm committed to living in Arkansas."

Visiting FDR's home in Hyde Park, 1992:

"The first house Hillary and I lived in had twelve hundred square feet. It could fit into one part of this house. The next house was even smaller. It had eleven hundred square feet. Then I lost, and we bought a big old house that I sold when I won again. We moved back into the mansion. I'm homeless. I'm a waif."

They were married in that first house October 11, 1975.

At their wedding:

"We are gathered here today to witness the joining of two people who'll be deeply involved in the political wars of 1976."

Hillary opted to keep her maiden name after they were married. It became an issue during the 1980 gubernatorial campaign:

"And, see, the interesting thing is, Hillary told me she was nine years old when she decided she would keep her own name when she got married. It had nothing to do with the feminist movement or anything. She said, 'I like my name. I was interested in my family. I didn't want to give it up.' And she was a young child when she decided that."

During his campaign for governor, some voters objected to Hillary's use of her maiden name:

"She understood that it was part of a picture that we had painted for the voters that made them feel alienated from us. And she said to me—I never will forget . . . I respected her so much for this, because she came in to see me, and she said, 'We've got to talk about this name deal.' She said, 'I couldn't bear it—if we're going to do this, let's try to win. I couldn't bear it if this costs you the election. It's just not that big a deal to me anymore.' "

She decided to take his name:

"People really liked it. Interestingly enough, they really liked it because it turned out to be that it was part of the picture that people had of us that we were smart, good, honest, and well-meaning, but that we spent too much time doing what we wanted to do instead of what they wanted us to do."

In 1978:

"She's just a hardworking, no-nonsense, no-frills, intelligent girl who has done well, who doesn't see any sense to extramarital sex, who doesn't care much for drink, who's witty and sharp without being a stick in the mud—she's just great."

Early Politicking

Both he and Hillary worked in the 1972 McGovern campaign.

———

To Billie Carr, liberal political activist, during the McGovern campaign:

"I'm gonna tell you something and you're gonna laugh. As soon as I get out of school, I'm movin' back to Arkansas. I love Arkansas. I'm goin' back there to live. I'm gonna run for office there. And someday I'm gonna be governor. And then one day I'll be callin' ya, Billie, and tellin' ya I'm runnin' for president and I need your help."

———

On Watergate:

"Too many congressmen did not speak up. If they had, I believe we would not be faced with the sad and dismal prospect of impeaching the president of the United States . . . the people of this country do not perceive Watergate as completely a party problem. One man could not have created all the trouble we have in the country today."

———

RUNNING FOR CONGRESS, 1974

His first campaign was a bid for Congress in 1974:

"Best campaign I ever ran. I just got in my little car and drove and had a hell of a time . . . It's what I like about politics."

———

In 1974 Clinton was invited to give the keynote address to the Democratic State Convention:

"We know that in every system of law, because men are frail and fall short of glory, justice must be tempered with mercy. But we want it remembered that, even for the favored few, mercy must be tempered with justice."

He lost the election.

———

He wrote to his opponent, J. P. Hammerschmidt:

"Congratulations on your victory yesterday. I hope you will consider the merit of the positive positions I took during the campaign. They grew out of the long months of discussions I had with our people. I wish you well in the next two difficult years. If ever I can be of service to you in your attempts to help the people of the Third Congressional District, please call on me."

———

ATTORNEY GENERAL, 1976

Campaigning in 1976 for attorney general of Arkansas:

"This morning as I drove up Highway 7 from Hot Springs in the breathtaking beauty of our Arkansas spring, I thought of all the long roads so many of us have walked together, up and down this river valley—not just through the main towns, but also to the hamlets of which so many others are dimly aware—to Houston, Casa and Adona; Havana, Briggsville and Chickalah; Coal Hill, Hartman and Lamar; Hector, Appleton and Dover and more. I know them all because they are home to me, because of you. I believe there is an unbreakable bond between us and have tried to keep faith with it . . . Now I need you once more to fight another battle. If you will do it, it will be an exhilarating reaffirmation of the work to which I have given the fullest measure of my time and strength and spirit."

"I believe that I can offer the background, experience, and interest in all the areas in which the attorney general's office must be interested."

———

He won this election and served as Arkansas attorney general until he ran for governor two years later.

The Gubernatorial Years

Running for Governor
1978

While campaigning for governor with Craig Smith, they visited a little Arkansas town, nothing but a crossroads and a grocery store. Clinton said:

"You know, this is the only grocery store, so everybody within ten miles must come by here. If I stay right here, within two days, everybody in this little area will know that I've been here."

———

When told he didn't look old enough to be governor, he replied:

"Well, I will by the time this campaign is over."

———

Victory speech, 1978:

"This election is fundamentally a tribute to the decency and judgment and hope of the people of Arkansas. I know the problems we face in the state and nation are complex and that people feel frustrated and thwarted and are prepared to believe the worst about politicians when they hear it. And in campaigns, they hear plenty. But I still believe that, beyond those of any other state, our people are devoted to the proposition that our bright future will not be realized if we turn against ourselves.

"I want you all to know that I will be prepared, that I will be frugal with your tax dollars, and that I will work as hard as I can to bring the finest people into government. I will try to be worthy of the enormous trust you have placed in me this evening."

———

1980

"Hillary keeps telling me I don't understand the modern world. I really should have been governor in the 1930s, when I could have stayed in the office doing all this good work and then could have gone out to see the people and talk about it . . . I am an old-fashioned politician. Oh, I can work myself up and give an effective, hard-hitting, punctuating speech, like at the Democratic National Convention, but I really like to go out and talk to the people and answer their questions."

———

This election he lost.

———

After his 1980 defeat for reelection as governor, he appeared to a joint session of the legislature:

"We pay less taxes than the people in any other state in the Union, not to mention the District of Columbia. Accordingly, we are at the bottom in the level of public services in nearly every category, from teacher salaries to higher education to unemployment compensation. There is but one answer—broadening the tax base—and the state will have to come to it, sooner or later, meantime settling for the barest minimums in services expected in the American society."

———

Looking back at his first term, he reflected:

"I had hoped in my first term as governor that I would be able to make a dramatic difference, but the economy finally caught up with us."

After losing the 1980 election, he asked voters:

"Remember me as one who reached for all he could for Arkansas."

———

"I learned the hard way that you really have to have priorities and make them clear to people. You have to win people over. And to do that, you have to spend some time listening to them."

———

He appeared on the steps of the Capitol the morning after his defeat:

"Hillary and I have shed a few tears for our loss of last evening, but we accept the will of our people with humility and with gratitude for having been given a chance to serve our state . . . I grew up in an ordinary working family in this state, was able to go through the public schools and become attorney general and governor and serve people in the way that I had always wanted to since I was a boy."

———

1982

He ran again in 1982:

"I made a young man's mistake. I had an agenda a mile long that you couldn't achieve in a four-year term. I was so busy doing what I wanted to do I didn't have time to correct mistakes."

———

"If you'll give me a chance to serve again, you'll have a governor who has learned from defeat that you can't lead without listening."

He won the governorship back in 1982 and thanked the Arkansas Education Association for its support:

"I think for the rest of my life I will look back on this election with a mixture of disbelief that it happened and with a profound sense of humility and gratitude for people like you who worked their hearts out and went the extra mile to do something that no rational person thought could be done."

1984

He ran again and was reelected in 1984:

"I'm going to run as if I were starting out as an unknown and as if I were behind. I enjoy this and I'm ready."

"Our administration will pursue an ambitious agenda for Arkansas's future, an agenda based on our commitment to economic growth, our commitment to excellence in education, and our commitment to increased security and stability for our people.

"Our education program has a simple goal: to retain the progress of the special session on education and build on it . . . We must not weaken the standards or repeal the testing laws."

From a September 25, 1996, speech at the Congressional Hispanic Caucus Institute Dinner:

"When I was running for reelection as governor of my home state in 1984, I went through a litany of things that I had done as governor—just kind of like I just did with you. And all I said—

and frankly, I thought it was a great speech—I was out in the country giving this speech on a country crossroads, and there was a man in overalls in the mountains of north Arkansas, in the Ozarks, leaning up against a tree—he'd always supported me, listening to this speech. I mean, I thought it was really great. I thought it was terrific.

"So after it was over I went up to him and I said, 'Well, what do you think.' He said, 'Well, that's a pretty good speech.' He said, 'I heard all that about what a good job you did.' But, he said, 'Now, after all, that is what we hired you to do and you did draw a paycheck every two weeks.' He said, 'This election is about what you're going to do if we give you a new contract, not what you did before.' And, in truth, that is what this election is about. And my record and the record of all those others who are running for office is really relevant only as an indication of what we will do in the future and whether our general view of the direction of our country is right or wrong."

1986

"I just can't conceive of any circumstances where I'll run again. I didn't mean it to sound ominous. I meant it to sound nice. Twelve years is a long time to serve."

In 1985 he was asked about running for president:

"It would be fun even if you lost. It would be a challenge to go out and meet the people and try to communicate your ideas and bring the different parts of the country together."

———

He announced he would run for reelection in 1986 for governor:

"I will stay the course. I have asked people of this state to commit themselves to a decade of dedication. Over and over again I have asked you to work for the future. Over and over again you have responded, and today I can do no less.

38

"I cannot ask you to stay the course if I am willing to leave office before our programs are fully implemented . . . I want to stay home and finish the job."

———

On his reelection 1986:

"I'm proud that [Hillary] made this walk with me tonight.

"I think when the history of our state is written no one will prove to have done more to advance the cause of our children and the future of this state than she has.

"In our one hundred and fiftieth year, I believe with all my heart our best years are ahead of us. The tough campaign is over, and now it's time for the hard work to begin on our programs and our opportunities. It's time for all of us to pull together as a family."

———

1988

The announcement on July 15, 1987: he would not seek the Democratic presidential nomination:

"My heart says no. Our daughter is seven. She is the most important person in the world to us and our most important responsibility. In order to wage a winning campaign, both Hillary and I would have to leave her for long periods of time. That would not be good for her or for us."

———

"Mentally I was one hundred percent committed to the race, but emotionally I wasn't."

———

39

"My head said so, and my heart said, 'It isn't right for you now.' Deep down inside, I knew that it was not the right time for me."

———

His nominating speech for Dukakis at the 1988 convention was not a success:

"I just fell on my sword. It was a comedy of errors, one of those fluky things."

———

Johnny Carson joked about his 1988 speech and later invited him on the "Tonight Show":

"It was not my best hour. It was not even my best hour and half."

———

1990

"Only two people before me had ever been elected to more than two terms, and only two people had ever served more than six years as governor. So I had already done ten. And to get elected for fourteen . . . I was afraid, too, that people might say—my popularity was very high in the state at the time. But I was afraid people might say, 'Give this guy a gold watch, he's done a good job—give him the gold watch!' "

———

Announcing his run for governor again, March 1, 1990:

"I must confess that one of the reasons I have been reluctant to face this day is the fire of an election no longer burns in me. The joy I once took at putting on an ad that answered somebody else's ad, that won some clever little argument of the moment, is long since gone.

"I've listened carefully to my friends and counselors around the country, but mostly just here at home. Some say, 'Leave while you're on top. Walk away from a nasty political campaign.' Others say, 'My God, you're only forty-three years old. Surely you're good for one more term.'

"In spite of all my reservations about the personal considerations, I believe that, more than any other person who could serve as governor, I could do the best job . . . We know there is always the problem of arrogance of power, and we are bending over backward to be as humble as we can in this campaign . . . In the end, I decided that I just didn't want to stop doing the job."

———

During the 1990 election campaign, he was again asked about his plans for national office:

"George Bush is at eighty percent in the polls.

"Do you think there's going to be a presidential race in nineteen ninety-two? Besides that, I'm doing what I'm interested in doing. I think all this election speculation is, again, your efforts to divert people's attention from the real issues so you'll have another story to write, and I think that's sad.

"I'm going to be governor four years. We're going to have a good four years, and we're going to have a great legislative session in nineteen ninety-one, I think."

———

"I will not run for president."

———

"I don't foresee any circumstances in which I can run."

———

41

"Will you guarantee to us that if reelected, there is absolutely, positively no way that you'll run for any other political office and that you'll serve out your term in full?"

"You bet! I told you when I announced for governor I intended to run, and that's what I'm gonna do. I'm gonna serve four years. I made that decision when I decided to run. I'm being considered as a candidate for governor. That's the job I want. That's the job I'll do for the next four years."

———

"In spite of all the talk of who is and who is not ambitious, I am the only person in this decade who has wanted only to be governor of Arkansas, who has never longed for the opportunity to run for any other job. When I had the chance to run for one other in 1987, I decided to stay here with you and finish this term because I believe in you and what we can make for you and your children and your grandchildren and our future together."

———

EDUCATIONAL STANDARDS COMMISSION

After being reelected in 1983 he appointed a commission to devise a set of minimum standards for schools. He appointed his wife to chair it:

"This guarantees that I will have a person who is closer to me than anyone else overseeing a project that is more important to me than anything else. I don't know if it's a politically wise move, but it's the right thing to do."

———

From his Inaugural Address, January 1983:

"We must dedicate more of our limited resources to paying our teachers better; expanding educational opportunities in poor and small school districts; improving and diversifying vocational and high technology programs; and, perhaps most important, strengthening basic education. Without competence in basic skills, our people cannot move on to more advanced achievement."

———

The part of the education plan most controversial was the requirement for teachers to take a competence test. He said:

"It is a small price to pay for the biggest tax increase in the history of the state and to restore the teaching profession to the position of public esteem that I think it deserves."

———

Teacher testing brought a higher rate of failure for black teachers and more criticism for Clinton's plan. On CBS TV's Face the Nation that failure rate was brought up and suggested to be discriminatory:

"I agree that would be discriminatory if the test was given once and then if you didn't pass it you couldn't be recertified . . . I believe the evidence is that black teachers can learn these skills and can do just as well as white teachers . . . Black children and poor white children in our state . . . have no other shot but the public schools to have a decent education and a decent opportunity in life. We're doing this for them."

———

He told the press that his proposed tax increase for education was:

"The most important thing I've ever tried to do. It's more important to me personally than whatever political consequences will come of it . . . It's something that's worth putting myself and whatever career I might have on the line for."

———

Parenthood

CHELSEA CLINTON

Chelsea Victoria Clinton was born on February 27, 1980.

After being cited for speeding while Hillary was pregnant, the governor joked that he'd name their daughter "Hot Rodham."

"One day when she was six, I picked her up, and she said, 'Dad, do girls sometimes have babies when they are not married?' I said, 'It's not the right thing to do, but it happens sometimes.' I asked her if she wanted to talk about it, and she said, 'No, I just wanted to know.' "

Opening Roundtable Discussion on Balancing Work and Family, June 24, 1996:

"You know, when Hillary and I were young parents and she had already spent many years studying all this—she took an extra year in law school to work at the Child Study Center when we were in law school so that she would know a lot about the impact of the law on children and their interests. And I'll never forget, one day I was working on something, working like crazy, and Chelsea was about a year old, and she said, you know all that stuff they tell you about quality time, she said it's about half not true. She said, 'Time counts; show up.'

"And I can remember a lot of nights when I would read my daughter to sleep and I would fall asleep before she would. And she would elbow me, and say, 'Dad, finish the book, finish the book.' But it meant something. Even the nights when I wasn't very good, you know, it meant something."

On the decision not to run for president in 1988:

"I promised myself a long, long time ago that if I was ever lucky enough to have a kid, my child would never grow up wondering who her father was."

Conversation with Memphis Commercial Appeal *reporter Joan Duffy in 1991:*

"Nobody gets two shots anymore. It doesn't work that way anymore. This is it. I either run and I either make it or I don't but this is it.

"If I wait four more years, Chelsea will be in high school. She'll be a senior in high school and she could stay here with friends or family or whatever and finish out high school here and then go off to college and have a relatively normal life. But if I do it now, if lightning strikes and I win, she loses me."

"We're sort of making it up as we go along. I think one of the things that has made Chelsea's life bearable as an only child is that we have done so many things together. I have driven her to school every day since kindergarten, unless I was away. The morning is our time."

"When I was home at night, I would always go in and put her to bed. We'd kneel down and say our prayers together, and then I would always either read her a book or tell her a bedtime story. And we developed these—I'm sick now that I didn't tape all of them—stories! I mean, hundreds and hundreds of stories. We had all these great characters we made up. I could have had another life as a children's book writer."

———

In 1992:

"I have to give more credit to her mother than to me. She has her mother's character and intelligence, and she looks like she's going to have my energy level. And if she gets that, she'll have the best of both worlds. She'll have a massive constitution to endure long years of effort. She'll have Hillary's character and intelligence. She'll be in good shape."

———

When asked "Why have kids?" he responded:

"Apart from the fact that it keeps civilization going—someone's got to do it—I think the experience of putting someone else first, constantly in a way that is full of joy even in the tough times, makes you a better person, a fuller person, more whole. I mean, I can't imagine what my life would have been like if I'd never become a father. I'm certain that I will have been a better person, better husband, better governor, better president, for having been a father. Parenthood ties you to the rest of life in a way and makes you less self-absorbed."

Campaign 1992

"I wouldn't mind running but I haven't made a decision. I'd like to be able to do it someday."

———

1991, still not running for president:

"Once there are four or five people running, the ones that aren't running won't be mentioned anymore. As long as nobody runs, everybody can be on the list. And it's kind of nice. It makes my mother happy to read my name in the paper."

———

In August 1991, he formed a presidential exploratory committee.

———

On October 3, 1991, he announced:

"All of you, in different ways, have brought me here today, to step beyond a life and a job I love, to make a commitment to a larger cause: preserving the American Dream, restoring the hopes of the forgotten middle class, reclaiming the future for our children.

"I refuse to be part of a generation that celebrates the death of communism abroad with the loss of the American Dream at home.

"I refuse to be part of a generation that fails to compete in the global economy and so condemns hardworking Americans to a life of struggle without reward or security.

"That is why I stand here today, because I refuse to stand by and let our children become part of the first generation to do worse than their parents. I don't want my child or your child to be part of a country that's coming apart instead of coming together."

"I am proudly announcing my candidacy for president of the United States of America.

"I promise an administration that will broaden opportunity for all Americans through better schools, more college-scholarship programs, generous tax breaks for the middle class, and a healthier economy.

". . . My style of government will expect more from all Americans—from the welfare recipients who I will want to see seek work, to the corporate executives who will face an angry president if they engage in the excesses of the 1980s.

"The change we must make isn't liberal or conservative. It's both and it's different. The small towns and main streets of our America aren't like the corridors and back rooms of Washington. People out here don't care about the idle rhetoric of 'left' or 'right' and 'liberal' and 'conservative' and all the other words that have made our politics a substitute for action. . . . We need a new covenant to rebuild America. It's just common sense. Government's responsibility is to create more opportunity. The people's responsibility is to make the most of it."

———

On the morning before he announced his candidacy for president, he jogged alone. When reporters and photographers approached, he waved them away:

"I don't know how many more mornings I'll have like this, and I wanted to spend this one like I normally do."

———

"I've been sort of at peace with myself in all this whirlwind. The worst that could happen to me is that I'd go home to my friends and my family and my wife and my work."

Introduced at a forum in New Hampshire as the smartest of the candidates:

"Isn't that a little like calling Moe the most intelligent of the Three Stooges."

――

"My answer to the Republicans is that in the last twelve years America has gone in the wrong direction and Arkansas in the right direction. It's pretty hard in a poor, rural state with no help from Washington to do that. My simple message is this: Politics is not about miracles; it's about direction. And the country's going in the wrong direction. Hire me."

――

Asked how he feels about being nominated:

"I feel very grateful to the people who made it possible and to the people here at home without whom I would not have been in a position to run. I feel humbled by it; it's an awesome responsibility. And I feel determined, as determined as I've been since I've begun this. There is a feeling, I think perhaps more intense among people my age and a little older, that this is a moment we have to try to turn the country around, revive it economically, reunite it, renew it."

――

During a Broadway for Bill Clinton fund-raiser, he said that while growing up in Arkansas . . .

". . . it never occurred to me that one day I'd be hobnobbing on Broadway with the cultural elite. To hear Dan Quayle tell it, I are one."

54

"I want to be a president for every man, woman, and child in this country. But that means we all have to be Americans again, not just getting but giving, not just placing blame but taking responsibility, not just looking out for ourselves but looking out for each other.

"I believe with all my heart and soul that Americans want to be part of a country that brings out the best in us, not the worst."

———

"This election is a clarion call for our country to face the challenges of the end of the Cold War, and the beginning of the next century."

———

"We must never let a blizzard of statistics blind us to the real people and the real lives behind them."

———

"I'm not out to soak the rich. I wouldn't mind being rich myself. But I do believe that rich people should pay their fair share of taxes. For twelve years, while middle-class incomes went down, the Republicans raised taxes on middle-class people. And while the incomes of our wealthiest people went up, their taxes were lowered. That's wrong, and the middle class needs a break."

———

At a campaign stop in Fort Worth, Texas:

"It will be nice for you not to have a president who has an accent. When you hear me talk and Mr. Bush talk, who's more like you?"

"On this last day of the campaign, we should take it to the limit one more time."

Victory speech, Old State House, Little Rock:

"I remind you again tonight, my fellow Americans, that this victory was more than victory of party. It was a victory for the people who work hard and play by the rules, a victory for the people who feel left out and left behind and want to do better, a victory for the people who are ready to compete and win in the global economy but now need a government that offers a hand, not a handout."

OPPONENTS

George Bush:

"I'd like to say to Mr. Bush, even though I've got profound differences with him, I do honor his service to our country. I appreciate his efforts and I wish him well. I just believe it's time to change."

"Tonight ten million Americans are out of work. Tens of millions more work harder for less pay. The incumbent president says unemployment always goes up a little before we start a recovery. But unemployment only has to go up by one more person before we can start a real recovery—and Mr. President, you are that man."

"He (Bush) took the richest country in the world and brought it down. We took one of the poorest states in America and lifted it up."

———

Ross Perot

"The Perot people share my view that the system is broke. Campaign-finance reform is part of the way to begin fixing it. We're gonna do it."

———

"I have to learn to describe what I've done in those kind of terms. My plan is an attack on political corruption and on economic stagnation. The difference is, if you ask me how I'm going to attack those things, I've got an answer. He is a very gifted sound-bite politician. And he is a good salesman—that is how he made a lot of his money, selling to the government. I'm also at a disadvantage because I'm an elected official. That turned out to be a negative [with] people who are fed up with politics as usual. Perot says, 'I'm a businessman, I have nothing to do with this,' which isn't so—he's been a Washington power player for twenty years."

———

On Perot's success:

"I understand it. The American people are disillusioned with both parties."

———

"I want to say, since this is the last time I'll be on a platform with my opponents, that even though I disagree with Mr. Perot on how fast we can reduce the deficit and how much we can increase taxes on the middle class, I really respect what he's done in this campaign to bring the issue of deficit reduction to our attention.''

———

Campaign Issues 1992

The Budget

''There's spending and there's spending. We're not spending this money on consumption, we're spending it on direct investment in ways that will promote jobs and economic growth. Certainly, [the Fed] shouldn't raise interest rates in the face of it. There is no reason to believe that this will spark a round of inflation.''

———

''I have shown we can balance the budget without retreating from our common ground on education, on health care, on the environment.''

———

The 1995 Budget:

''This budget's dead on arrival when it comes to the White House. If the price for any deal are cuts [to Medicare and Medicaid] like these, then my message is 'No deal.' ''

———

''This budget debate is about two very different futures for America; about whether we'll continue to go forward under our motto, *E pluribus unum*—out of many one; whether we will continue to unite and grow together, or whether we will become a more divided winner-take-all society.''

———

"A balanced budget that reflects the best of both parties, the best of our values, and will pass on to the next generation a stronger America. That is within our grasp. We should get it done now. And I believe we will get it done in the near future."

———

The 1996 Budget:

"We could balance the budget in about fifteen minutes. In order to do that, some of the differences between me and the Congress over some of these issues will have to be taken out of that budget agreement and deferred for the election. But that's what elections are for."

———

"And I said in the beginning, let me say again: If the objective is to get a seven-year balanced budget that Congress says is balanced, we can do that. If the objective is to get a modest tax cut, we can do that. If the objective is to dismantle the fundamental American commitments through Medicare and Medicaid, or to undermine our obligations in education and the environment, I will not do that.

"That is basically where it is."

———

Change

When asked, "What is this election finally going to be decided on?"

"I think it will be a race of change against the fear of change, of hope against fear in general, or new ideas against a more comfortable past.

"It always takes more courage for people to change than to stay

59

with a proven course, even if it's a failed course. My own conclusion, what brought me into this race, was that the country has to change.

"If the American people decide that we must do some things very differently than we've been doing for the last twelve years, then they will vote for Bill Clinton and Al Gore."

———

"Profound and powerful forces are shaking and remaking our world, and the urgent question of our time is whether we can make change our friend and not our enemy."

———

First Inaugural Address, January 20, 1993:

"My fellow citizens:

"Today, we celebrate the mystery of American renewal.

"This ceremony is held in the depth of winter. But, by the words we speak and the faces we show the world, we force the spring. A spring reborn in the world's oldest democracy, that brings forth the vision and courage to reinvent America.

"When our founders boldly declared America's independence to the world and our purposes to the Almighty, they knew that America, to endure, would have to change.

"Not change for change's sake, but change to preserve America's ideals—life, liberty, the pursuit of happiness. Though we march to the music of our time, our mission is timeless.

"Each generation of Americans must define what it means to be an American."

———

"A lot of the changes we need in this country have to come from the inside out."

Children

"It is a long, long way in this country from . . . me at the age of six holding my great-granddaddy's hand to a condition where children on the streets of this city don't know who their grandparents are and have to worry about their own parents' drug abuse. I tell you, my friends, if we cannot make common cause with those kids, we cannot keep the American Dream alive for any of us."

———

From his acceptance speech:

"I want to say something to every child in America tonight who's out there trying to grow up without a father or a mother. I know how you feel . . . If other politicians make you feel like you're not a part of their family, come on and be part of ours."

———

"A strong sense of security is very difficult to achieve in life unless you know when you're little that you're the most important person in the world to someone."

———

"Not so long ago, kids grew up knowing they'd have to pay if they broke a neighbor's window playing ball. I know; I did it once. They knew they'd be in trouble if they lied or stole because their parents and teachers and neighbors cared enough to set them straight. And everybody knew that anybody who committed a serious crime would be caught and convicted and would serve their time in jail. The rules were simple, the results were predictable, and we lived better because of it. Punishment was swift and certain for people who didn't follow the rules, and rewards of America were considerable for those who did.

"Now, too many kids don't have parents who care. Gangs and drugs have taken over our streets and undermined our schools. Every day we read about somebody else who has literally gotten away with murder. But the American people haven't forgotten the difference between right and wrong. The system has. The American people haven't stopped wanting to raise their children in lives of safety and dignity, but they've got a lot of obstacles in their way."

———

"Being engaged with a child, I think, makes you a better person, enhances the value and meaning and depth of what you do with the rest of your life."

———

"We cannot renew our country when within a decade more than half of our children will be born into families where there is no marriage.

"We cannot renew our country when thirteen-year-old boys get semiautomatic weapons and gun down nine-year-old boys—just for the kick of it.

"We cannot renew our country when children are having children and the fathers of those children are walking away from them as if they don't amount to anything. . . .

"We cannot renew our country unless more of us are willing to join the churches and other good citizens who are saving kids, adopting schools, making streets safer.

"We cannot renew our country until we all realize that governments don't raise children, parents do—parents who know their children's teachers, turn off the TV, help with the homework, and teach right from wrong—can make all the difference.

"Let us give our children a future."

". . . people who deny that culture is a force are wrong. The states in this country with the lowest incarceration rates also have the highest high-school graduation rates, and they often don't spend the most money. There are almost no poor children in families with two parents in the home. So if I could just wave a magic wand and make this problem go away, I would never have another kid in a home where there weren't two parents until the child reached a certain age so that then the child could take care of himself or herself. That would be a wonderful thing if that could be done."

―――――

The End of the Cold War

"Thanks to the unstinting courage and sacrifice of the American people, we were able to win the Cold War. Now that we have entered a new era, we need a new vision and the strength to meet a new set of opportunities and threats. We face the same challenge today that we faced in 1946—to build a world of security, freedom, democracy, free markets and growth at a time of great change.

"Given the problems that we face at home, we must first take care of our own people and their needs. We need to remember the central lesson of the collapse of communism and the Soviet Union: We never defeated them on the field of battle. The Soviet Union collapsed from the inside out—from economic, political, and spiritual failure."

―――――

"The collapse of communism is not an isolated event: It is part of a worldwide march toward democracy whose outcome will shape the next century. If individual liberty, political pluralism, and free enterprise take root in Latin America, Eastern and Central Europe,

Africa, Asia, and the former Soviet Union, we can look forward
to a grand new era of reduced conflict, mutual understanding, and
economic growth. For ourselves and millions of people who seek
to live in freedom and prosperity, this revolution must not fail.''

———

Community

To Democratic Leadership Conference, 1991:

''We're here to save the United States of America. Our burden is
to give the people a new choice rooted in old values. A new choice
that is simple, that offers opportunity, demands responsibility, gives
citizens more say, provides them responsive government, all because we recognize that we are community. We're all in this together, and we're going up or down together.''

———

To Hispanic Caucus Institute Board and Members, September 27,
1995:

''In Florida last week, Governor Lawton Chiles said that the central
question of our time was whether we were going to be a community
or a crowd. The Hispanic community in America has always been
a community, always tried to live by family values, not just talk
about them. Now, a crowd is a group that occupies the same piece
of land, but really has no particular connection to one another. And
so they elbow and shove and go to and fro until the strongest win
and others are left behind.

''A community is a group of people who occupy the same piece
of land, and recognize their obligations to one another; people who
believe they're going up or down together; people who believe
they should help protect children and do honor to the elderly and
help people make the most of their own lives; people who believe
in freedom and responsibility; people who believe that we have an

obligation to find common ground and sometimes to do the right thing because it's right, even if it's unpopular in the short run.

"And in this period of change, as we move out of an industrial to an information society, out of the Cold War into the global economy, that is what we need more than ever before—the values of your family and your community and your work."

State of the Union Address, January 24, 1995:

"We all gain when we give. We reap whatever we sow. That's at the heart of the New Covenant: Responsibility. Citizenship. Opportunity. They are more than stale chapter headings in some remote civics book. They are the virtues by which we can fulfill ourselves and our God-given potential—the virtues by which we can live out the eternal promise of America, the enduring dream of that first and most sacred covenant: 'That we hold these truths to be self-evident, that all men are created equal. That they are endowed by their Creator with certain inalienable rights. And that among these are Life, Liberty and the Pursuit of Happiness.'

"In the twelve years that I served as the governor, when I had the opportunity not only to go to every community in my state, but from time to time to travel throughout the country, I saw a modern example of what the framers of the Constitution intended when they set up state governments, and they basically devolved a certain amount of authority throughout our country. They wanted the states and, ultimately, communities to be laboratories of democracy. And they thought, the people who set our country up, that once in any laboratory a solution to a problem was found it would be like science, that that then would be adopted and people would go on to another set of problems.

"What I think is happening in our country is that nearly every serious challenge we face has been dealt with brilliantly by somebody, somewhere—whether it's in education, or in dealing

65

with the crime problem, or you name it. The one place where their laboratory of democracy problem fell down is that its human affairs are not like science, and very often, even though things are working well, they're not adapted, adopted, embraced as they should be.

"So I think that all of you who are struggling and working to find ways to mobilize the energies not only of your communities, but willing, then, to see it spread across the country are doing the most important thing you could be doing because it's the second half of what the framers of the Constitution knew we'd have to do in order to meet all the challenges of the future."

———

Crime

Promoting an anticrime package at the Ohio Peace Officers Training Academy in London, Ohio, February 15, 1994:

"We've got to have more . . . officers on the street . . . people who know their neighbors and their children, understand when there are problems . . . and do things that are necessary to keep crime from happening in the first place."

———

On the Signing of the Crime Bill, September 12, 1994:

"One of the reasons that I sought this office is to get this bill because if the American people do not feel safe on their streets, in their schools, in their homes, in their places of work and worship, then it is difficult to say that the American people are free."

———

The Deficit

At the 1992 presidential debate, on how the national debt had affected him personally:

"Well, I've been governor of a small state for twelve years. I'll tell you how it's affected me . . . I see people in my state, middle-class people—their taxes have gone up and their services have gone down while the wealthy have gotten tax cuts . . . In my state, when people lose their jobs, there's a good chance I'll know them by their names. When a factory closes, I know the people who ran it. When the businesses go bankrupt, I know them. And I've been out here for thirteen months meeting . . . with people like you all over America, people that have lost their jobs, lost their livelihood, lost their health insurance."

"The American people know, I think overwhelmingly they know, that we've got to get control of the deficit, we've got to get control of health-care costs, we have to increase investments so that we'll have jobs and incomes, so that we can compete."

On the joys of deficit reduction:

"The United States doesn't borrow so much money. We have more of your tax money to spend on the education of your children, or on developing new jobs, or on health care. We keep interest rates down, and it's easier for you to borrow money in the private sector, so you create more jobs."

"It's the Economy, Stupid!"

From a 1980 article "A Governor Speaks to the Alienated Americans" by Bill Clinton:

"This is a painful time of transition of our nation. The economic arrangements, the cheap energy, the abundant natural resources, the lack of foreign competition on which our stability and prosperity depended for years are gone and they are gone forever. We were brought up to believe, uncritically, without thinking about it, that our system broke down in the Great Depression, was reconstructed by Franklin Roosevelt through the New Deal and World War II, and would never break again. And that all we had to do was to try to reach out and extend the benefits of America to those who had been dispossessed: minorities and women, the elderly, the handicapped, and children in need.

"But the hard truth is that for ten long years through Democratic and Republican administrations alike, this economic system has been breaking down. We have seen high inflation, high unemployment, large government deficits, the loss of our competitive edge. In response to these developments, a dangerous and growing number of people are simply opting out of our system.

"As a matter of common fairness, you ought to ask upper-income people to pay more for what they get. But it's more symbolic than real. The real money is in reducing poverty so you reduce the number of people making claims. And then to do something about health-care costs."

———

"Now we must understand, as we never have before, that our national security is largely economic. The success of our engagement in the world depends not on the headlines it brings to Washington politicians, but on the benefits it brings to hardworking middle-class Americans. Our 'foreign' policies are not really foreign at all . . . We can no longer afford to have foreign and domestic policies. We must devise and pursue national policies that serve the needs of our people by uniting us at home and restoring America's greatness in the world."

———

"We need a national economic strategy as well as a human-development strategy that recognizes we are living in a world in which what people earn depends largely on what they can learn and whether their economics are organized for change.

"So the three central ideas in my economic policy are:

"One, emphasize education and training, not just of our children but also of our adults.

"Two, give new incentives to the private sector to invest in this economy.

"Three, think a lot about organizing to make change our friend instead of our enemy."

———

"We meet at a special moment in history, you and I. The Cold War is over; Soviet communism has collapsed, and our values—freedom, individual rights and free enterprise—have triumphed. And yet just as we have won the Cold War abroad, we are losing the battles for economic opportunity and social justice here at home. Now that we've changed the world, it's time to change America."

———

Gays in the Military

For the first time in the memory of [gay] activists, the presumptive nominee of a major political party openly appealed for homosexual support:

"What I came here today to tell you in simple terms is, I have a vision and you're part of it."

"I don't know if we had anybody openly gay, but we had gay people in town and everybody knew who they were. Every now and then, there were snickers behind their back, but there was no overt persecution of them. See, this is more about saying than doing, this whole thing. It's not so much whether they're gay or not, but whether you can own up to being gay and still have your job or serve your country."

———

"I think people should not be asked to lie if they're going to be allowed to serve. The question is not whether they should be there or not. They are there. The narrow question of this debate is . . . Should you be able to say that you're a homosexual if you do nothing wrong? I say yes."

———

Excerpts from the announcement on January 29, 1993, on the suspension of the Pentagon's ban on gay service personnel:

"The issue is not whether there should be homosexuals in the military. Everyone concedes that there are. The issue is whether men and women who can and have served with real distinction should be excluded from military service solely on the basis of their status. And I believe they should not.

"The principle on which I base this position is this: I believe that American citizens who want to serve their country should be able to do so unless their conduct disqualifies them from doing so. Military life is fundamentally different from civilian society. It necessarily has a different and stricter code of conduct, even a different code of justice.

"Nonetheless, individuals who are prepared to accept all necessary restrictions on their behavior, many of which would be intolerable in civilian society, should be able to serve their country honorably and well.''

Hillary's Role

Asked if the first lady should have a policy role in the White House:

"If I were to be elected president, I would like Hillary to be involved, to be a real voice for America's children, to try to change some of our policies to promote child-rearing and stronger families. She has, after all, worked on that for more than twenty years now in her association with the Children's Defense Fund. There's not a handful of people in this country who have done as much work as she has on this issue.''

"Our life is very much a partnership. Our public endeavors, we do in common. And I always say that my slogan might well be: Buy one, get one free.''

"She's extraordinarily able and would be very much involved.''

"She always thought that the right kind of Democrat would have an opportunity to be elected in '92—always. I mean, from the beginning of [George Bush's] term, when he took office she told me that. And when he got up to seventy percent and then ninety percent or whatever in the polls after the Gulf War, she never wavered in her conviction that '92 was a good year for the right sort of Democrat to challenge the established orthodoxy of the Democratic Party, and also challenge the incumbent president. It was amazing. And I've got to give her credit for that. That's one where her instinct was right, and I didn't feel that way for the longest time . . . She thought that in '88 we still had a reasonably good economy and that the adverse consequences of Reaganomics were not fully apparent to most voters; and that by '92 they would be. And she always believed that. And she never changed her opinion . . . It was quite amazing. She was really right about that. She had a sense about it. Once I got out and around the country in '91, I began to feel it . . . but she sensed it just from her reading of events and her feel for it."

―――

"I have never known a person with a stronger sense of right and wrong in my life. And I do not believe for a moment that she has done anything wrong . . . If everybody in this country had a character half as strong as hers, we wouldn't have half the problems we've got today."

―――

Hillary was widely criticized for the famous "staying home and baking cookies"* quote:

"It gave a totally false impression of who she was. She was defending her right to practice law and be the wife of a governor."

―――

*"I suppose I could have stayed home and baked cookies and had teas, but what I decided to do is fulfill my profession. The work that I have done as a professional, a public advocate, has been aimed . . . to assure that women can make the choices . . . whether it's a full-time career, full-time motherhood, or some combination."

"I think she really feels bad [about how her comments] were read. What she was saying is she resented Jerry Brown or anybody else trying to force her to make those choices on how the role of a first lady in the state or a nation might be defined. The way the remarks were read was a slam at women who chose to be homemakers and mothers. And she did not mean it that way, but I think she would concede that they could be read that way. I believe and she believes that the most important job in society today is child-rearing. I've seen her tell young women who were on the professional track in law school, 'If your mother stayed home, honor that.' Of all the things that have happened in this campaign, I think that's among the saddest for me because the minute I read it, I thought, 'People are going to think something that is different from what she has preached for a decade.' "

The Middle Class

"Do you know that in the 1980s, while middle-class income went down, charitable giving by working people went up, and while rich people's income went up, charitable giving by rich people went down? Why? Because we live in a country which had an ethic of get it while you can and to heck with everybody else."

"There has been a sort of class welfare in America in the last twelve years. I don't want to make class warfare. I just want the rich to pay their fair share. I still want it to be possible for people to make a lot money in America the old-fashioned way, by putting people to work and producing goods and services. I definitely am trying to reunite the poor and middle class and remind the middle class that the large majority of the poor are the working poor."

"Too many middle-class Americans don't trust us to defend our national interests abroad, to put their values into our social policy at home, or to take their tax money and spend it with discipline."

"I'm going to change the way the tax burden has been dumped on the shoulders of the middle class. And I'll ask the very wealthy to pay their fair share for a change.

"I'm going to hold down health-care costs, before they bankrupt our families, our businesses and our state and federal governments. I'll make health care a right, not a privilege, for every man, woman, and child in America."

From acceptance speech, July 16, 1992:

"And so, in the name of all those who do the work, pay the taxes, raise the kids and play by the rules—in the name of the hardworking Americans who make up our forgotten middle class, I proudly accept your nomination for president of the United States.

"I am a product of that middle class. And when I am president you will be forgotten no more."

Responsibility

"We must do what America does best: offer more opportunity to all and demand more responsibility from all. It is time to break the bad habit of expecting something for nothing, from our government or from each other."

"As we offer opportunity, we must also demand responsibility. The problems of our society will only be solved if there is an upsurge of personal responsibility—if individuals take it upon themselves to meet their obligations, do the right thing, and give something back to those around them."

Scandals and Crises

"Like other people, I have had crises in my life, personal crises, personal failures, the sense that I had let myself and others down, the sense that maybe I'd never be the person God wanted me to be."

On handling crises:

"I think there's a point at which you have to let it go, because you have to go on to other things. But of course it affects you personally. And we talk about it when we come home from work. In some ways, it's more difficult here, because you kind of work where you live. That's nice in some ways because it gives our family a lot more access to one another. But it's just impossible to leave everything at the office.

"We try to spend some time every night after we go to bed reading, talking, doing something that has nothing to do with your work, because if you don't, it's very hard to get replenished for the next day."

"The Character Issue"

"I believe the best way for me to demonstrate my character is to make sure people know the whole story of my life and my work and my family and what I'm fighting for in this election."

———

"Character is a journey, not a destination."

———

"I do not pretend to have met a standard of perfection. The people of the South . . . know that the measure of character in politics can never be perfection, because if it were, no one could pass."

———

"Most people deep down inside always want to do better, and most people down deep inside know that we're all imperfect, that even the very best lives are a daily lifelong struggle for integrity, for continuing to do better.

"I feel that way about character. It's about the continuing search for belief and conviction and action and the ability not to disappoint yourself as well as others. It's a lifelong process. And I think that people know that different folks have different difficulties to deal with, but they identify with people who seem to be on the journey."

———

"The Marriage Question"

When asked by a reporter, "Have you ever committed adultery?" he replied:

"If I had, I wouldn't tell you."

———

He acknowledged that their marriage had "difficulties" and that:

"If the standard is perfection, I can't meet it."

———

"I am the only person I am aware of to ever run for president to come . . . with my wife to say that we were really proud our marriage was still together, because we had difficulties . . . and we worked through it."

———

Early in the 1992 campaign, "the question" began to come up:

"What you need to know about me is we have been together for almost twenty years and have been married almost sixteen, and we are committed to our marriage and its obligation, to our child and to each other; we love each other very much.

"Like nearly anybody that's been together twenty years, our relationship has not been perfect or free of difficulties. But we feel good about where we are. We believe in our obligations. And we intend to be together thirty or forty years from now, regardless of whether I run for president or not.

"And I think that ought to be enough."

———

Steve Kroft on 60 Minutes, *January 26, 1992:*
"I think most Americans would agree that it's very admirable that you have stayed together, that you've worked your problems out, that you seem to have reached some sort of an understanding and an arrangement . . ."

———

"Wait a minute. You're looking at two people who love each other. This is not an arrangement or an understanding. This is a marriage. That's a very different thing.

"You know, I have acknowledged wrongdoing. I have acknowledged causing pain in my marriage. I have said things to you tonight and to the American people from the beginning that no American politician ever has. I think most Americans who are watching this tonight, they'll know what we're saying, they'll get it, and they'll feel that we have been more candid. And I think what the press has to decide is: are we going to engage in a game of gotcha? You know, I can remember a time—and it was sad—when a divorced person couldn't run for president. And that time, thank goodness, has passed. Nobody's prejudiced against anybody because they're divorced. Are we going to take the reverse position now—that if people have problems in their marriage or things in their past which they don't want to discuss, which are painful to them, that they can't run?"

———

"I think the American people who saw that *60 Minutes* program saw two people who love each other and respect each other and are very proud they didn't give up on their marriage."

———

Scandals

"I just didn't pop out of a box yesterday . . . [Americans] have a right to be worried about being lied to. But there's not a single shred of evidence in my public career that I've been dishonest. Even people who dislike me would tell you that I wouldn't take a nickel to see the cow jump over the moon. I'm getting a little sick and tired about being asked those kinds of questions."

"The only relevant questions are questions of whether I have abused my office, and the answer is no."

___

Gennifer Flowers

> Asked to describe his relationship with Gennifer Flowers on 60 Minutes, January 26, 1992:

"Very limited, but until this, you know, friendly, but limited. I have—I met her in the late nineteen seventies when I was attorney general. She was one of a number of young people who were working for the television stations around Little Rock. And people in politics and the people in the media knew each other then, just as they do now. She left our state, and for years I didn't really hear from her or know what she was doing. Then she came back—I don't know—sometime a few years ago and went to work again for the state. So that's how—that's who she is. . . . She was an acquaintance. I would say a friendly acquaintance."

___

On 60 Minutes:

"It was only when money came out, when the tabloid went down there offering people money to say that they had been involved with me that she changed her story. There is a recession on. Times are tough, and I think you can expect more and more of these stories as long as they're down there handing out money."

___

Paula Jones

Statement issued regarding Paula Jones:

"I have no recollection of meeting Paula Jones on May 8, 1991, in a room at the Excelsior Hotel. However, I do not challenge her claim that we met there and I may very well have met her in the past. She did not engage in any improper or sexual conduct. I regret the untrue assertions which have been made about her conduct which may have adversely challenged her character and good name. I have no further comment on my previous statements about my own conduct. Neither I nor my staff will have any further comment on this matter."

———

Whitewater

"We did nothing improper. Old story."

———

Accepting a special counsel on Whitewater:

"I need to get on with the business of my presidency."

———

"I lost money, and I didn't take a tax deduction, and people think I'm a crook."

———

From a press conference, March 8, 1994:

"This is not what I was hired to do . . . I was hired to be president."

———

"There is no credible evidence and no credible charge that I violated any criminal or civil federal law eight or nine years ago when most of these facts that are being bandied around are discussed."

———

From a press conference, March 31, 1994:

"Many people around America must believe that Washington is overwhelmingly preoccupied with the Whitewater matter. But our administration is preoccupied with the business we were sent here to do for the American people. None of this in the light of history will be as remotely important as the fact that by common consensus we had the most productive first year of presidency . . . of anyone in a generation. That's what matters—that we're changing people's lives."

———

On the investigations:

"Do I feel terrible about the completely innocent middle-class people who have been wrecked financially by this? I certainly do. But I didn't abuse them, and it's high time that the people who abuse have to take responsibility for what they do. I will take responsibility for my actions, but the people who have . . . abused them should be held accountable by somebody, somewhere, sometime.

"Meanwhile, I'm going to help them pay their legal bills if it's the last thing I ever do and I stay healthy."

———

"I show up for work every day. The American people ought to feel good about me. They spent $30 million or something and there has been not a single solitary shred of evidence of any wrongdoing on my part. I feel good about it."

———

The Presidential
Years

VICE PRESIDENT AL GORE

On his choice of Al Gore for vice president:

"The man standing beside me today has what it takes to lead this nation from the day we take office."

———

"I looked around the country for people I thought had real ability, real character, real achievement. I found that there were a remarkable number of things where we had the same passions, like the economy and children's issues, and areas where he knew things that I didn't just by the nature of his job, and where he had a real important perspective that I thought would be important for my presidency, like in defense and arms control and foreign policy and issues that are important for the whole world, like his environmental positions."

———

From acceptance speech, July 16, 1992:

"I am so proud of Al Gore. He said he came here tonight because he always wanted to do the warm-up for Elvis. Well, I ran for president this year for one reason and one reason only: I wanted to come back to this convention and finish that speech I started four years ago."

———

When asked why he hadn't gotten the high-tech vice president to install some virtual reality games at Camp David to replace its old-fashioned pinball machines:

"He's virtual reality. I'm reality."

———

"Al Gore is doing for the federal government what he did for the macarena. He is removing all the unnecessary steps."

———

"I tell people all the time that Al Gore is the most important vice president in history and he has done more than anybody else ever has, really I'm bragging on myself, you know, because I think I showed such good sense in selecting him. And besides that, the more he does, the more likely it is I can play golf a couple times a month."

———

1996:

"I remember when I was trying to decide what sort of person I wanted to ask to run with me for vice president and I made up my mind I wanted somebody who was smarter than I was—that left a large field to pick from—someone who was philosophically in tune with me, someone who would work like crazy, and someone who knew things I didn't know. And I read *Earth in the Balance,* and I realized it was a profoundly important book by someone who knew things I wanted to learn. And we have learned a lot and done a lot together over the last four years."

———

Tipper Gore

"I want to say about Tipper Gore, you know, we share the same birthday; therefore, we are under the same—but she's younger than I am. Therefore, we are under the same sign. We have the same sort of enthusiasm about life. And she is always irreverently puncturing my balloon."

INAUGURATION

Asked about nerves on Inaugural day, January 20, 1993:

"None of that. Really, I was surprised by how relaxed I felt. Maybe it was because I got along with President Bush. I don't know what it was, but I felt very relaxed. You know, I had wanted the Smith Choir to sing, wanted Marilyn Horne to sing, wanted Billy Graham there. I had personally picked Maya Angelou, from my state, to give the poem. It was all just rocking along, and I felt real good about that speech when I went to bed last night. I felt that we had pared it down as well as we could."

WASHINGTON, D.C.

Comparing Little Rock to Washington:

"It's just not the same. It's just bigger and deeper and more complex here. I could short-circuit a lot of processes and always knew it was going to be all right. I have much greater respect now for trying to let our economic team work through a problem before I take a position, letting our national-security team work through a problem, and really rely on the people we put in these staff positions to have an orderly development of process."

From his Inaugural Address, January 1993:

"This beautiful capital, like every capital since the dawn of civilization, is often a place of intrigue and calculation. Powerful people maneuver for position and worry endlessly about who is in and who is out, who is up and who is down, forgetting those people whose toil and sweat sends us here and pays our way."

"There are more big egos doing more conniving over the most petty things that don't have anything to do with the country."

_____

"This town is gripped with people who are self-righteous, sanctimonious, and hypocritical."

_____

Democratic Governors' Association Dinner, February 5, 1996:

"It was so cold in Washington for these last two weeks, I had to have a break last weekend, so I went to New Hampshire. Well, anyway, I got outside the Beltway. For those of you who live here, you'll be happy to know that I not only got a good dose of old-fashioned American values, I saw in action the fine art of snow removal . . ."

"To be fair to the people here in Washington, D.C., who have that responsibility, Washington is still viewed by many people as sort of a Southern city. I mean, we have a half inch of snow, they close every school within fifty miles. And the kids like it, but it's not so great for the economy."

_____

On the 1996 book Primary Colors: A Novel of Politics *written by "Anonymous" about the 1992 campaign:*

"I must say, I admire the publisher and the author. It's the only secret I've seen kept in Washington in three years."

_____

Asked when it really hit him that he had actually won the White House, he told about the morning after the election:

"[Hillary] looked at me, and I looked at her, and we just started laughing, like 'Can you believe that this happened to us?' "

———

"I'll wake up every day in the White House with the idea that it's not my house; it's your house. I am nothing more than a temporary tenant and your chief hired hand."

———

To employees at Silicon Graphics in California, February 2, 1993:

"When we took office, I walked into the Oval Office—it's supposed to be the nerve center of the United States—and we found Jimmy Carter's telephone system.

"Then we went down into the basement, where we found Lyndon Johnson's switchboard. True story—where there were four operators working from early morning till late at night—literally, when a phone call would come . . . they would pick up a little cord and push it into a little hole. That's today, right?"

———

Shortly after his inauguration, giving a friend a tour of the White House:

"Don't let it fool you. It's the crown jewel of the federal prison system."

———

"We redid the little kitchen upstairs in the White House. And oftentimes, when it's just the three of us, we eat our meals in the kitchen. Hillary and I had dinner there last night. I try to have breakfast with Chelsea. She often will ask me questions about various things that are going on."

Asked whether he's startled by the questions Chelsea asks:
"No, not anymore."

THE PRESIDENCY

"The lack of confidence in our leaders is our number one problem. I mean to change that if I'm elected, because unless you restore the country's belief in its government and its faith in the pronouncements of the president, you'll never be able to get done any of the tough things the next president is going to have to do."

"I think I underestimated the importance of the president's voice, just being able to speak about these issues in a coherent, clear, and forceful way . . . The opportunity to speak turned out to be an action in itself because it seems to galvanize and mobilize the energy and the concentration of nations."

"A president is not America's chief mechanic. You know I didn't get hired to fix everything in that sense. I got hired to do what I'm now trying to do, to set forth a vision."

THE NOMINATING PROCESS

"There are two big problems with it. Unconventional people are too big targets and the process is entirely too long and bureaucratic. We've had some conversations with some of the people who worked on personnel with President Bush, for example, to discuss it. I just now talked to some people in town here about whether there is some way next year maybe I could ask a group of people, equally divided between Republicans and Democrats, to take a look at just what has become of the whole nominating process. If you take the [Supreme Court Nominee Robert] Bork case where I filed testimony against him, I worked for sixty hours myself personally on that. However, I liked him personally, and I was outraged that they looked into the movies he checked out and things like that. I mean, he's an interesting, unconventional man. There ought to be some interesting people in public life in America."

———

"First of all, it takes too long to get anybody appointed. People who are independent and who have led interesting lives may be able to get elected to public office but may not be able to get appointed to anything. It's just ridiculous. And thoughtful people in both parties recognize it. I'm trying to think of a device we can employ next year to get a good, fresh bipartisan look at the whole appointments process."

———

Lani Guinier

On Lani Guinier's nomination as Assistant Attorney General for Civil Rights, later withdrawn:

"At the time of the nomination, I had not read her writings. In retrospect, I wish I had."

———

"I love her . . . If she called me and told me she needed $5,000, I'd take it out of my account and give it to her, no questions asked."

———

Leon Panetta

Leon Panetta was appointed Director of Management and Budget. He had criticized Clinton's economic proposals during the campaign. Questioned about this:

". . . I'm going to give him a chance to teach me some math."

———

Ron Brown

On choosing Ron Brown for Commerce Secretary:

"I am grateful to Ron. A lot of times you and my mother were the only believers."

———

Joycelyn Elders

On Surgeon General Joycelyn Elders:

"When you have someone who is outspoken and energetic like she is, there are going to be times when she'll be outspoken and energetic in a way that I don't necessarily agree with. But I certainly stand behind her foursquare as surgeon general. I think she's done a good job, and she's beginning to really focus the country on a lot of these health problems."

Rodney Slater

"I can say that he was recommended by more people from more places in more ways for this job than any person for any position I have ever seen. And in spite of that—I am confident that he will be a superb and successful Secretary of Transportation."

___

ON BEING PRESIDENT

Asked about being elected:

"I felt like the dog that chased the pickup truck. I got it, now what am I going to do."

___

To reporters before leaving Little Rock:

"There have to be ways for the president to stay in touch with the pulse of America. You can't let the security bubble shut you down."

___

"I do not promise to be a perfect president. I will make some mistakes, because unlike the guy who's in there now, I'll do something."

___

After his first trip on Air Force One:

"It's a lot better than Air Elvis."*

*Referring to his campaign plane.

Describing how his presidency would be different:

"Don't people understand? It's going to be more fun."

―――

"I don't know that anyone feels adequate to it in the beginning. I think the genius of democracy is the idea that most people can do most jobs when they have to, and I think it's important to be really respectful of the challenges, but still to believe that they can be met."

―――

"I don't have to have this job. I like it, and I wanted it. But I didn't take this job not to change things. That's what I want, and that's what I think we Democrats, with some Republicans, can do. I'm willing to take the risk, and I hope you'll take it with me."

―――

December 13, 1993: *"One of the things that is said about your presidency is that it's been a roller-coaster ride. Do you think that's a fair assessment?"*

"At one level, I do. Part of it is growing pains, learning pains, while we were trying to move very quickly to push the agenda of change. But I think there's also been a constancy to it. We've had this immensely successful year in the Congress. We have begun to change the country and change the way government works and to make it more responsive to the interests of ordinary Americans."

On perks:

"I like Camp David 'cause there's great bowling alleys there and because there is a driving range.

"Camp David also has pinball machines. You know, young people all use PacMan and all those things, but older guys like me, we still remember pinball machines. There are two pinball machines at Camp David where I can indulge all my teenage fantasies. You ever play those pinball machines? I actually have a lot of fun."

———

Asked the best thing about living in the White House:

"The best perk is that there is a movie theater."

———

June 11, 1995:

"Let me just close by saying this: I wouldn't trade places with anybody in any other country. I get to represent you around the world. And with all of our problems, the diversity of America, the power of our entrepreneurial system, the resources and resolve of our people, we're still in better shape for the next century than any other country in the world. And don't you ever forget it."

———

October 9, 1995:

"The first two years I knew exactly [what] I wanted to do and I went about doing them. And I was obsessed with doing them . . . And I would have been better served, I think, and the country probably would have been better served . . . if we had done slightly less, if people had understood the big picture more. And the president, in a way, has to impart the big picture."

———

New Hampshire College, Manchester, New Hampshire, February 17, 1996:

"And I want to tell you, make no mistake about it, there's one thing I can do that none of you can do—I can go abroad to represent all of us. And when I do, it is a feeling I can't even put into words for you, because I'm no longer Bill Clinton, and I'm not even really the president. You just become the United States. And you realize what a very great country this is—what we stand for and what we can do."

———

August 30, 1996:

"It is the most rewarding thing in the world for a citizen of our country, who loves our country and believes in the promise of its people, to be president. To look back on the last four years and to go out here as I did on the train ride, or on this bus trip, and you look into the eyes of people and you go through these crowds and somebody will say, I've got a home because of one of your programs; I've gotten a job since you were here; I'm on one of your college loans; I'm an AmeriCorps student.

"When you see how the country is changing for the better, it's immensely rewarding."

Asked if he ever gets used to it:

"Well, I never have a time when I'm not proud to be here, and I don't feel a certain sense of awe about it."

January 27, 1997:

"I feel driven in the sense that I am ever more mindful of each passing day, that there is less time to work on this enormous project that the American people gave me to do over this eight years."

POLICIES AND PLANS

"The American people get sick of words and words and words, people showing how they feel and how their hearts bleed, and then nothing ever happens. One of the reasons for the embedded cynicism in this country is that they have been inspired by leaders over and over again, only to have nothing happen. So it's all very well for people to make fun of policy proposals and ideas, but the job of people in public life is not simply to inspire, it is to act, to do, to change life."

"I want a country where people are coming together across the lines of race and religion and income. I know we can do better. It won't take miracles, and it won't happen overnight, but we can do much, much better if we have the courage to change."

"I want to have a team established that can hit the ground running. I want one of those great hundred days in which Congress would adopt my health-care and education policies, my energy and economic initiatives, and where the private sector would become engaged in a whole new partnership to make this country great again."

"We're going to have to have no sacred cows except the fundamental abiding interest of the American people."

———

"I want my Cabinet to be more reflective of the American population by race and gender than any previous Cabinet. But no token appointments."

———

New Hampshire College, Manchester, New Hampshire, February 17, 1996:

"We are living in a world dominated by world markets for goods, for services, and for money. And what that means is that there are incredible new opportunities in this world for Americans, more than at any time in the history of the country, for those who are prepared to take advantage of them. But those who aren't prepared to take advantage of them, or those who have the misfortune of being downsized, it is not a rosy picture.

"What we have to do today is not to reverse the policies of the last three years. We are moving in the right direction. What we have to do is to bear down until every American has the opportunity to succeed. And we have to do it together."

———

National Service

During the 1992 campaign, Clinton proposed a college-loan program, available to all, repaid as a percentage of income over time or with two years' service in a "Domestic Peace Corps":

"We could educate a generation of Americans and help solve our people problems here at home. It would be the best money we ever spent."

"I want my national service plan to pass; that will open the doors of college education to millions of Americans."

———

"National service is an idea as old as America. Time and again our people have found new ways to honor citizenship and match the needs of changing times.

"Abraham Lincoln's Homestead Act rewarded those who had the courage to settle the frontier with the land to raise a family.

"Franklin D. Roosevelt's Social Security Act ensured that Americans who work a lifetime can grow old with dignity.

"Harry S Truman's GI Bill rewarded the service of my father's generation, transforming youthful veterans into an army of educated civilians that led our nation into a new era.

"For my generation, the reality of national service was born thirty-two years ago, when President John F. Kennedy created the Peace Corps.

"At its peak, the Peace Corps enrolled only sixteen thousand volunteers, yet it changed the way a generation of Americans look at themselves and the world."

———

From a speech to AmeriCorps Volunteers, Dallas, Texas, April 7, 1995:

"But this age and time has its own problems. If anybody had ever told me that we'd have as many children born out of wedlock, I wouldn't have believed that. If anybody had ever told me we'd have as many single mothers raising little children in poverty, I would not have believed that. We have new problems and new challenges. And the only answer to it is for people in the community to take responsibility for themselves and for each other, and

98

to have the chance to pull themselves up and work their way out. What did you say? That you wanted a hand up, not a hand down. That's as good a way to say it as I can imagine. That's what AmeriCorps is all about."

———

Second Americorps Swearing-in ceremony, October 12, 1995:

"At a time when, once again, we are asking ourselves whether we are too divided in our perceptions of reality and our attitudes toward all the things that are going on in America to be a real community, the members of AmeriCorps put the lie to all of that. They show us once again that if you can just get good people together, no matter how different their backgrounds are, and you give them a chance to share common values and to work on a common problem, or to seize a common opportunity, and you give them a chance to do it together, day in and day out, they will change everybody's preconceived notions of what is possible in America. They will prove, once and for all, again in this age, that the American idea is a universal idea; that the notion of personal responsibility, the notion of opportunity for everybody, the notion that we're all better and stronger when we work together than when we are divided, that those things are universal; that they are rooted in a fundamental truth about human nature, and that there is no power like it anywhere. That's what these young people in Ameri-Corps prove day in and day out."

———

Health Care

1992 campaign:

"We should provide health care to the elderly when they need it— before they spend themselves into poverty. Our senior citizens should make their own choices about how to spend their health-

99

care benefits. In Arkansas, we created a program that gives seniors the right to take money which used to be used . . . for nursing-home care and spend it on home health care, personal care, transportation to senior centers, hiring a nurse, or attending an adult day-care center. I want a federal health system that gives seniors all over the country the same choices.''

———

"A Clinton administration will treat affordable, quality health care as a right, not a privilege. Employers and employees will either purchase private insurance or opt to buy into a high-quality public program. My goals also include universal workplace coverage, protection for small businesses, improved preventative and primary care, expanded long-term care, and intensified health education.

"The only way to secure national health-insurance coverage for everyone, however, is to bring costs down.''

———

"Health care is one of the areas where we must contain the paper explosion. Under the Clinton plan, the costly billing, coding, and utilization-review functions that currently govern most provider-payments systems would be replaced by a simplified, streamlined billing system. The billions fueling our health-care bureaucracy would be better spent on providing better care for all Americans.''

———

"My mother was a nurse-anesthetist. I grew up hanging around hospitals. The first people I ever looked up to were people who provided health care—doctors and nurses. I watched surgery as a boy and didn't get sick from the blood or anything. I've always been fascinated with it and cared a great deal about it.''

"Government occasionally does do something right in health care. I think the Medicare program is generally conceded to be fairly well run and some of its cost-control programs have worked quite well. They would have worked better had they been part of an overall managed-competition plan. Government's capable of fixing financing mechanisms and administratively simplifying things."

———

"The plan we envision would still allow people to choose their doctors, would still leave the private practice of medicine alone, would give doctors much more free time to work with their patients and less time on paperwork and regulation. The American Medical Association issued a rather cautiously optimistic statement this week, and I think you'll see an awful lot of physicians for this plan."

———

Asked if he is staking his presidency on health care:

"Well, I don't know about that. I believe it's terribly important because of the millions of Americans who are riddled with insecurity. I have worked for better health care all my public life. I am encouraged at the spirit that has pervaded this discussion in the last several weeks. We really are moving toward a great national debate in a way that is not couched in terms of who's going to win, who's going to lose. Republicans and Democrats are all talking to each other. We've got the health-care providers and the advocates talking to each other. We've got almost four hundred members of Congress signed up for this two-day Health Care University, which is an astonishing affirmation of the importance of public debate here. So the outcome is terribly important. It's one reason I ran for president."

Asked if he is staking his marriage on it:

"It's been a joy, actually. We started out working together very closely when we were young at law school. When we both taught at law school we loved working together. When I was governor we worked together on educational matters a lot, and we worked together on health matters. But it wasn't as consuming as this. This is the first time since we got together that we've been able to work so closely over such a sustained period on an issue, and it's been a joy. Both of us care a lot about this, and both of us have been involved in health care for a long time. Both of us see that if this happens in a very meaningful way, then all the work we did to get here, and all the work we've done here, and all the things we've done in our public life would really seem that it was all very much worth doing."

The Health Security Act:

"I've thought about this until my brain aches."

Asked why he put Hillary in charge of health care:

"She's better at organizing and leading people from a complex beginning to a certain end than anybody I've ever worked with in my life."

"When we started this process, I knew a lot more about it than she did. Now she knows a lot more about it than I do.

"When I launched our nation on this journey to reform the

health-care system I knew we needed a talented navigator, someone with a rigorous mind, a steady compass, a caring heart. Luckily for me, and for our nation, I didn't have to look very far."

"The politicians have it, the wealthy have it, the poor have, [and] if you go to jail you've got it. Only the middle class can lose it."

State of the Union Address, January 25, 1994:

"From the day we began, our health-care initiative has been designed to strengthen what is good about our health-care system: the world's best health-care professionals, cutting-edge research and wonderful research institutions, Medicare for older Americans. None of this— none of it should be put at risk.

"But we're paying more and more money for less and less care. Every year fewer and fewer Americans even get to choose their doctors. Every year doctors and nurses spend more time on paperwork and less time with patients because of the absolute bureaucratic nightmare the present system has become. This system is riddled with inefficiency, with abuse, with fraud, and everybody knows it.

"In today's health-care system, insurance companies call the shots. They pick whom they cover and how they cover them. They can cut off your benefits when you need your coverage the most. They are in charge.

"What does it mean? It means every night millions of well-insured Americans go to bed just an illness, an accident, or a pink slip away from having no coverage or financial ruin. It means every morning millions of Americans go to work without any health insurance at all—something the workers in no other advanced country in the world do. It means that every year, more and more hardworking people are told to pick a new doctor because their boss has had to pick a new plan. And countless others turn down better jobs because they know if they take the better job, they will lose their health insurance.

"If we just let the health-care system continue to drift, our country will have people with less care, fewer choices, and higher bills."

———

"Rampant medical inflation is eating away at our wages, our savings, our investment capital, our ability to create new jobs in the private sector, and this public Treasury. If we do nothing, almost one in every five dollars spent by Americans will go to health care by the end of the decade."

———

On Hillary and health care:

"Every president who's ever tried to solve the health-care problem has failed at it. Roosevelt couldn't do it. Johnson couldn't do it. I knew that she would be able to inspire and motivate and organize people, and she did. I think she did a fine job, but we didn't get there. We failed. And so I think she took a lot of unfair hits."

———

At the White House Office of Women's Initiatives "At the Table" Meeting, October 8, 1996:

"Essentially, we got beat, Hillary and I did, on the health-care thing."

———

"In my acceptance speech in Chicago and across America I have called upon Congress to take the next steps. And yesterday congressional leaders answered this call in two very important ways. First, Congress agreed to tell insurance companies, newborns and their mothers deserve at least forty-eight hours in the hospital.

"In 1970, the average length of stay for an uncomplicated delivery was four days. By 1992, it was two days. Today, a large and growing number of insurers refuse to pay for anything more than twenty-four hours, and some even recommend release as early as eight hours after delivery. That's risky and wrong. And it can have severe health consequences for new babies, including feeding problems, dehydration, brain damage, and stroke.

"We've all heard heartbreaking stories like the family in New Jersey sent home after twenty-four hours, whose baby died twenty-four hours after that from an infection that would have been detected and treated in a hospital. Doctors, not rigid insurance-company rules, should decide when a new baby goes home."

———

"Congress agreed that it's time to ensure that people who need treatment for mental illness will get the treatment they need without discrimination. From now on, insurance companies will have to set the same limits for mental illness that they set for physical illness—no more double standards."

———

Second Presidential Debate, San Diego, California, October 16, 1996:

"One of the things that I tried to do was to make sure that everybody in the country who was under a managed-care plan should at least have three choices of plan and would have the right to get out without penalty every year. That's not a government takeover. That's like the Family and Medical Leave law—it just tries to set the rules of the game.

"I'm strongly in favor of a federal bill to repeal any gag rules on providers. In other words, I believe that doctors should not be able to be kicked out of managed-care plans just because they tell the patient what they need and what more expensive care options might be. If we're saving money and managing resources better, that's a good thing. If we're saving money and depriving people of care, that's a bad thing. A good place to start is to say, no managed-care provider can gag a doctor and kick the doctor out of the managed-care plan for the doctor telling a patient you need a more expensive test, you need a more expensive procedure, your health requires it."

———

Reinventing Government

"When I talk about reinventing government, I mean it, big time."

———

Accepting the nomination, 1992:

"We've got some changing to do. There is not a program in government for every problem. And if we really want government to help people, we've got to make it work again.

"We offer our people a new choice based on old values. The choice we offer is not conservative or liberal; in many ways, it's not even Republican or Democratic. It is different. It is new. And it will work."

———

"I never viewed government as the enemy. I think it has to be radically reformed so that the taxpayers feel it serves them."

———

"Federal agencies need the kind of restructuring that major corporations have undergone, which means compressing middle management, pushing decisions down to front-line workers and using data processing instead of paper pushing. The best companies do it by attrition, not by layoffs.

"I believe government can both care about people and be careful with their money."

———

First major address to Congress, February 1993:

"We must begin to make government work for ordinary taxpayers, not simply for organized interest groups."

———

Interview with Time *magazine,* 1993:

"You asked me earlier what else had surprised me. I'm a little chagrined to admit this because it shouldn't surprise me, having been a governor for twelve years. But one of the things that has struck me since I won this election is that there are a huge number of people who work for the federal government and know about all these things I care about. Many of them have been out there for years, and nobody has ever asked them for their opinion. There are a lot of really gifted, devoted people who ought to be given a chance to hook into this future we are trying to build."

———

"It is time for government to demonstrate . . . that we can be as frugal as any household in America."

———

"Our founders established this great country under a constitution that limits government. Mostly, it limits what government can do to private citizens and gives us a lot of elbow room to think what we please and say what we please and go where we please and worship God as we please. It also limits government in other ways, divided it at the state and local, as well as the national level—the president, the Congress, the courts. But it was set up to allow all of us to pursue life, liberty, and happiness. And it was set up with enough flexibility so that over time we could have the kind of government that we needed as a people—not the kind of people that the government needs, but the kind of government that we need as a people."

———

"I believe the purpose of government is not to expand bureaucracy, but to expand opportunity. I do not believe government is inherently good or bad. I believe there are some things we need government to do, because private markets, as good as they are, do not solve all the problems of a free society. And I find it amazing that anybody could question whether I have core beliefs."

———

"We have sixteen thousand fewer pages of government regulations. My favorite, because I'm from Arkansas, was when I showed up I realized there was a whole page of government regulations on what grits were. And I could have just given the name of four hundred people they could teach something to, and they could say this is grits or it's not."

———

"I think the American people are torn about what role government ought to play. They say they can't stand big government and they want less of it—but they have huge aspirations for it. After so many years of stagnant income and rising social problems, they want immediate results. But the best solutions can take a long time to work because the problems developed over a long time, and because making progress on them depends not only on government but also on people taking more personal responsibility."

———

"I have always believed that the role of government was not to undermine self-reliance, but to reinforce it; not to weaken families, but to help them grow stronger; not to do what could be done at the grass-roots community level or at the state level, but to empower states and communities to do what they ought to do.

"Government is our neighbors and friends helping others pursue the dreams we all share: to live in peace, provide for ourselves and our loved ones, give our children a chance for an even better life."

———

"I believe the most important things in all of our lives are the personal things—that your individual life, your family life is clearly the most important thing. I believe many things have to be done at the grass-roots level by people in the private sector, by religious and community organizations and civic organizations, by local government. But I believe the national government is not your enemy;

it is your servant, your partner. I believe it does take a village to raise our children and build our future."

"I thought the era of big government was over, and then I saw all these people here."

Second Inaugural Address:

"The preeminent mission of our new government is to give all Americans an opportunity—not a guarantee, but a real opportunity—to build better lives."

FAMILY LIFE IN THE WHITE HOUSE

"We're a little family, but we're a powerful one."

When Hugh Rodham died on April 7, 1994, *Clinton told* Parents *magazine:*

"I must tell you, I miss Hillary's father a lot. I really love her parents. They've been wonderful to me. And that's been one of the great blessings of our life together. You know, the parents of one person are often skeptical of the other in the marriage. I used to write sort of mental marks in my mind when I knew I was making progress with Hillary's father—marks toward worthiness, you know."

On meeting author John Grisham, who told Clinton that they were distantly related:

"Well, if I'm going to have relatives falling from the sky, I may as well have one rich one."

———

Hillary Rodham Clinton, First Lady

"I'm not sure people aren't right when they say Hillary is the one who ought to be running. You know, we like each other. You can watch me watch her speak sometimes, and I've got the Nancy Reagan adoring look. I think she's one good argument for voting for me."

———

"There's a poll saying that forty percent of the American people think Hillary's smarter than I am. What I don't understand, is how the other sixty percent missed it."

———

"I thought when we married maybe someday we'd practice law together. The first jobs we had, we were at the same job when we started out. We were both teachers in the law school at the University of Arkansas and since I've been [in the White House], we do have more time together and some of it is quite romantic in spite of all the pressures of the moments, and, I know this may sound hokey, but my happiest times here are when we go down alone to the movie theater with two boxes of popcorn."

———

"I am most proud of how she's raised Chelsea. I say that because from the first time I met her, I knew she would be a great lawyer. She's achieved a lot of things I'm proud of, from the time we were on the mock trials together in law school to the Watergate Committee to leading educational reforms here in Arkansas. I always knew she could do that. But the fact that she was able to have this incredibly full professional and public life and still be a wonderfully successful person as a good mother and wife, and grow over the years is, I think, her greatest achievement."

————

"Hillary has just gotten better, like old wine."

————

"We talk to each other during the day, sometimes up to a dozen times. Sometimes, I just pick up the phone. I just get lonesome in there sometimes, if I've taken a good whipping or something. You know, the one thing I never did before I came here is have lunch regularly. I always just worked through lunch four out of five times unless I had a speech or some working lunch. Now, it's really quite nice to be where I can see Hillary."

————

"She knows a lot about education and training and how that relates to the business community, because she's had a lot of major corporate experience. She knows a lot about children's issues and health-care issues, and I expect she'll be very active there."

————

"It's my job, it's my duty to the American people, to take advantage of the most talented people I can find. She certainly qualifies there, and I would be derelict in my duty if I didn't use her in some major way within the confines of what is proper."

———

Asked what sort of president he thought Hillary would be:

"Oh, she'd be great at it. But I don't think she'd ever run—not in a hundred years."

———

Why?

"Because she just always told me that the one thing she was not interested in was being in elected office—and she's always said that publicly."

———

"[Hillary] always had very mixed feelings about running for public office. She loves public service—she's always loved it. And she's always been happiest, I think, doing it. But, primarily, she's never seen herself as an elected official."

———

"She has a visceral, intuitive, almost irrepressible desire to try to find and do the right thing."

———

"I could cite you chapter and verse over twenty years plus now that I have known her when it would have been very easy for her to take a shortcut, to do something else when she has unfailingly done the right thing.

"I'm just telling you, the American people can worry about something else. Her moral compass is as strong as anybody's in this country, and they will see that."

———

"It's just not accurate to portray her as somebody who is out there on the left wing of this administration."

———

"I have been blessed with a wife who has a loving, caring, and courageous heart, who is herself a wonderful mother, and who has dedicated herself to making our nation a better place. The smartest thing I've ever done was convincing Hillary Rodham to marry me."

———

"A lot of my public life has been our life. We've done it together."

———

"Our working relationship has been the same since we've been married."

———

Asked if his wife would make a good president:

"She'd make a good anything. I've never seen any job that I didn't think she could do well. She'd be good at anything."

". . . Ladies and gentlemen, it is wonderful to be here. Thank you for all these wonderful signs—'Students For Clinton,' 'Teachers For Clinton,' 'Cardinals and Clinton,' 'Seniors For Clinton.' There's one that says, 'I'm from Haynes, Arkansas.' I'm from Hope, Arkansas. Good for you. My favorite one is that one back there that said, 'I'd vote for anyone smart enough to marry Hillary.' Thank you very much."

Address to the Democratic National Convention, Chicago, Illinois,
September 15, 1996:

"Tonight, tonight, I thank the city of Chicago, its great mayor and its wonderful people for this magnificent convention.

"I love Chicago for many reasons, for your powerful spirit, your sports teams, your lively politics, but most of all for the love and light of my life, Chicago's daughter, Hillary. I love you."

Chelsea Clinton

1992:

"I want this to be a good move for our daughter. Hillary and I have talked about that a lot. Chelsea has had a good life here. It's exciting for her now. She's smart and pretty grown-up for her age and interested in it, but I want her life to unfold without being destructively impacted by this."

"It used to be that the mornings were the best time for Chelsea and me. At least I would always take her to school. But now that's not practical. I mean, I could do it, but it would be terrible for her. It's no fun when you're thirteen to be taken to school by a caravan. But now we can at least meet at home at night."

———

On the choice of a private school for Chelsea:

"We made a decision based on what we thought would give her the best chance to have a normal childhood in a world in which the children of people like me aren't treated normally."

———

"If I hear that Chelsea's come home from school, I just walk over there and see what she's doing. If I work until 7:30 P.M., I can go home to dinner at 7:30 P.M. and have three hours with Chelsea and Hillary.

"And I think that parenting is the most important job in this society and the one that has been neglected most. I think having people with families work here makes for a place more in touch with the real world. So I'm concerned about it. Next year will be a more livable environment for our people. I'm determined to see that it is."

———

"What we try to do is to protect her by just letting Chelsea be a completely private person. In past years she was just another little girl in *The Nutcracker*. So this year it may be different. I hope that it is not too much different, because she doesn't want it to be any different."

———

116

In answer to the question "Who is she more like, you or Mrs. Clinton?":

"I think she's more like Hillary, though in some of her habits she's more like me. She's incredibly energetic. She likes to have large numbers of her friends over. She hates to go to bed, which is just the way it was when I was young—and still sometimes am.

"She and I like a lot of the same things. We like action movies, we like sporting events. But down deep, she's a lot like her mother. She has her mother's character, her mother's real strong sense of what's right or not. She has a core about her that's so much like Hillary was the first time I met her, a long time ago."

———

"She has an extraordinary social conscience, which both her mother and her grandmother have. And she's very disciplined. She's extremely ethical, deeply religious. And she's sort of no-nonsense in a lot of ways. I like that about her."

———

"The thing she and I both miss is that we used to go out together, just the two of us, and be left alone. We'd go to a movie or to a bookstore, or to get a frozen yogurt. That's tougher now, if not downright impossible."

———

"It's kind of nice. She's been a teenager for a whole year, and we haven't become completely irrelevant to her yet."

———

"I've always been conscious that every experience and every day with my daughter is a gift."

"I tell my daughter I love her every day of her life, and I frequently tell her I'm proud of her."

——

"I used to help her with her math, but she's getting a little too advanced for me."

——

"She's had as normal a childhood as you can in the White House."

——

When asked how he feels about Chelsea's dates:

"Well, you know, I have met a lot of her young friends. And I think, after they have been here a time or two, they feel pretty comfortable around us—and around me. It is okay with me if they do not feel entirely comfortable. Whenever she goes out, she tells us when she expects to be home. We say yes or no, and we kind of negotiate it that way. Whenever she goes out, I wait up until she comes home, even though the Secret Service is with her. Maybe it is old-fashioned, but I just—I can't go to bed until she is there."

——

"You're very proud—and justly so—of Chelsea. What of yourself at sixteen do you see in her?"

"I think she's smarter than I am and in much better physical condition that I was at sixteen; but I see more of her mother in her than me. She has her mother's great sense of character and concern. But she's a lot like me in that she's got a great sense of compassion and feeling for other people. Even though she's not at all interested in politics herself, she cares a lot about public life and the impact of public decisions on people's lives."

———

Socks

Written statement from Clinton to photographers who used catnip to lure the First Cat-elect Socks into camera range:

"Special note to all press from the highest authority: don't touch the cat again."

———

Portland, Oregon, September 1996:

"And finally, we want to use technology to open government to people more. Today, I want to announce that the White House Home Page, which many of you have already used on the Internet—see that sign 'Portland wants Socks'—even my cat has a place on our home page."

———

"If you just think about the Internet, four years ago when I took the oath of office as president, about the only people who knew about the Internet were nuclear physicists. Today my cat has his own home page and Web site. I stop and shake hands with schoolchildren; they don't know very much about me, but they have been conversing with Socks on the Internet."

———

PEOPLE

Ron Brown

> *At Dover Air Force Base in April 1996 when the dead returned after the plane crash that killed Commerce Secretary Ron Brown and thirty-four others:*

"Life is more than what we know. Life is more than what we can understand. Life is more than, sometimes, even we can bear. But life is also eternal."

———

Senator J. William Fulbright

> *During the years at Georgetown, he got a clerical job at Senator J. William Fulbright's office:*

"I got the job despite the fact that I was a nobody, that my family had no money and no political influence . . . simply nothing else at all."

———

"He made me believe that there was no intrinsic conflict between being an intellectual and being a public official."

———

Billy Graham

"When I was a small boy, about twelve years old, Billy Graham came to Little Rock, Arkansas, to preach a crusade. That town was torn apart by racial conflict. Our high schools were closed there, and there were those who asked Billy Graham to segregate his audience in War Memorial Stadium so as not to roil the waters.

"And I'll never forget that he said—and it was in the paper— that if he had to speak the word of God to a segregated audience,

120

he would violate his ministry, and he would not do it. And at the most intense time in the modern history of my state, everybody caved, and blacks and whites together poured into the football stadium. And when the invitation was given, they poured down together, down the aisles, and they forgot that they were supposed to be mad at each other, angry at each other, that one was supposed to consider the other somehow less than equal.

"And he never preached a word about integrating the schools. He preached the word of God and he lived it by the power of his example. And one young boy from a modest family for a long time thereafter took just a little money out of his allowance every month and sent it to Billy Graham's Crusade. And I've lived with that all my life."

―――

Jesse Jackson

"Jesse is right in the sense that we're kidding ourselves if we believe we can rebuild the fabric of life . . . if there is no work."

―――

Barbara Jordan

"I, too, remember the first time I ever heard Barbara Jordan speak, and I thought maybe God is a woman after all."

―――

Dr. Martin Luther King, Jr.

"Martin Luther King, Jr. personified the best of America. I was a seventeen-year-old high-school student in Arkansas when Dr. King helped lead the March on Washington. I listened carefully to the words as Dr. King articulated his dream for the country. His powerful vision inspired us all because it was full of hope and deeply rooted in the promise of America. When I got a copy of the speech, I read it over and over until I memorized it. Five years later when Dr. King was gunned down in Memphis, Tennessee, I was a student at Georgetown University in Washington, D.C., as the city erupted into flames. Since that time, I have felt we all have a special obligation to protect Dr. King's flame of hope from being blown away by the winds of prejudice and senseless violence. In the memory of this man who gave his life to the nonviolent struggle for justice, we all must keep the dream alive.''

Jacqueline Kennedy Onassis

''More than any other woman of her time, she captivated our nation and the world with her intelligence, her elegance and her grace. Even in the face of impossible tragedy, she carried the grief of her family and our entire nation with a calm power that somehow reassured all the rest of us.''

Willie Mays

''He loved to play baseball, not just to hit, and he always seemed to be happy. He lit up the place. He could smile, and it was like lights coming on in my television set. I loved him.''

Tip O'Neill

State of the Union Address, January 25, 1994:

''As we gather to review the State of the Union, I recall the memory of the giant who presided in this Chamber with such force and grace. Tip O'Neill liked to call himself 'a man of the House.' And he surely was that. But— even more—he was a man of the people, a bricklayer's son who helped build the American middle class. Tip O'Neill never forgot who he was, where he came from, or who sent him here.

"We, too, must remember who we are, where we come from and who sent us here."

Rosa Parks

Twenty-sixth Annual Congressional Black Caucus Foundation dinner, September 14, 1996:

"Even one of the photographers said, 'You're lovely, Ms. Parks.' You guys never say anything like that to me."

Pope John Paul II

November 1995:

"A few weeks ago, I was privileged to spend some time with His Holiness, Pope John Paul II when he came to America. At the very end of our meeting, the Pope looked at me and said, 'I have lived through most of this century. I remember that it began with a war in Sarajevo. Mr. President, you must not let it end with a war in Sarajevo.'"

General Colin Powell

August 1993:
Asked what he's looking for in the next Chairman of the Joint Chiefs of Staff:

"A good one. Colin Powell was great."

1996:

"If he had run, it would have been the first time since McClellan ran against Lincoln that a commanding general ran against a president he had served. I mean, think about it."

Elvis Presley

"Most people in my part of the country really liked him because he was from Tupelo, Mississippi, right across the river. He was the cultural rage of my childhood—before the Beatles."

When Elvis died, he called the hospital where his mother worked and spoke to a nurse:

"I have a message for mother that I don't want her to hear from anybody else."

When asked whether he would choose "Elvis" as his Secret Service name:

"I could do worse. Then all the Elvis fans could say, 'Well, Elvis is alive.' It's just another thing I could do for the country."

Yitzhak Rabin

State funeral of the prime minister of Israel, Yitzhak Rabin, Har Herzl Cemetery, Jerusalem, Israel, November 6, 1995:

"Your prime minister was a martyr for peace, but he was a victim of hate. Surely we must learn from his martyrdom that if people cannot let go of the hatred of their enemies, they risk sowing the seeds of hatred among themselves.

"I ask you, the people of Israel, on behalf of my nation that knows its own long litany of loss, from Abraham Lincoln to President Kennedy to Martin Luther King, do not let that happen to you."

———

American-Israel Public Affairs Committee policy conference, April 28, 1996:

"When I was in Jerusalem last month, I placed a small symbol of the extraordinary bond of solidarity between the United States and Israel on the grave of my friend Prime Minister Rabin. It was a little stone from the South Lawn of the White House where the first accord with the Palestinians was signed. I put it there in keeping with the Jewish tradition that says one must always add to the memories of those who have died and never detract from them.

"Well, it falls to us to add more to the memories of all those who have given their lives for Israel's security and for the hope of peace. And we must do this not only with stones, but in kind. We must build a peace as hard and real as any stone. And in so doing, we will add to the memory of every martyr and validate the sacrifice of every martyr, and give meaning and breath and life to the dreams of so many who have gone before."

"That is my vision to you and my pledge. And I say to you, and especially to you, I will do everything I can to help us achieve it together."

———

Jackie Robinson

Celebration of the fiftieth anniversary of Jackie Robinson's entry into major league baseball:

"In the days when Jackie Robinson broke into baseball, someone had to make a decision that this racial prejudice was a stupid, dumb

125

thing. But . . . he still had to play baseball. He had to maintain his dignity, waiting for that chance and never knowing for sure it was going to come."

———

"Every American should say a special word of thanks of Jackie Robinson and to Branch Rickey and to the members of the Dodgers team who made him one of their own and proved that America is a better, stronger, richer country when we all work together and give everyone a chance."

———

Mother Teresa

At a 1994 National Prayer Breakfast at which Mother Teresa delivered an antiabortion plea:

"I was so moved by the profession of faith and the experiences of Mother Teresa that almost anything that any of us could say would be anticlimactic."

———

October 1, 1996:

"Today I am delighted to sign a resolution conferring Honorary United States Citizenship on Mother Teresa. . . .

"To be an American citizen, is to share certain fundamental values: That we have a duty to help others live up to their God-given promise, that we have a responsibility to build up and reinforce the bonds of community, that we have an obligation to extend our hands to those who cannot always help themselves.

"By this measure, Mother Teresa is already an American citizen. I am proud to make it official."

EVENTS

Fiftieth Anniversary of D-Day Celebrations

At D-Day celebrations in Italy, he called on:

". . . the sons and daughters of the world they saved to honor the memory of those who fought in World War II."

US National Cemetery above Omaha Beach, Colleville-sur-Mer, France, June 6, 1994:

"We know that progress is not inevitable. But neither was victory upon these beaches. Now, as then, the inner voice tells us to stand up and move forward. Now, as then, free people must choose.

"Fifty years ago, the first Allied soldiers to land here in Normandy came not from the sea, but from the sky. They were called Pathfinders, the first paratroopers to make the jump. Deep in the darkness they descended upon these fields to light beacons for the airborne assaults that would soon follow. Now, near the dawn of a new century, the job of lighting those beacons falls to our hands.

"To you who brought us here, I promise, we will be the new pathfinders, for we are the children of your sacrifice."

"They were the fathers we never knew, the uncles we never met, the friends who never returned, the heroes we can never repay. They gave us our world. And those simple sounds of freedom we hear today are their voices speaking to us across the years."

127

"Today, many of them are here among us. Oh, they may walk with a little less spring in their step and their ranks are growing thinner, but let us never forget—when they were young, these men saved the world."

Independence Day

"On Independence Day, we celebrate the birth of the first and greatest democracy of the modern era.

"The ideals embodied by the Declaration of Independence have served as a guide for our nation and as an inspiration for people around the world."

Two hundredth birthday celebration of Youngstown, Ohio, and one hundred and fiftieth birthday celebration of Mahoning County, Ohio, July 4, 1996:

"Somebody joked with me—I don't know if any of you have seen this new movie *Independence Day*—but somebody said I was coming to Youngstown because this is the day the White House got blown away by space aliens. I hope it's there when I get back."

Ceremony for Boys' and Girls' Nation, the East Room, July 18, 1996:

"Very interesting, don't you think, that this movie, *Independence Day,* is becoming the most successful movie ever? Some say it's because they blew up the White House and the Congress—and that may be. But, you know, you see story after story after story about how the movie audiences leap up and cheer at the end of the movie when we vanquish the alien invaders, right? I mean, what happened? The country was flat on its back, the rest of the world was threatened, and you see all over the world all these people have all of a sudden put aside the differences that seem so trivial once their existence was threatened, and they're working together all over the world to defeat a common adversary."

———

Oklahoma City

"The bombing in Oklahoma City was an attack on innocent children and defenseless citizens. It was an act of cowardice, and it was evil. The United States will not tolerate it. And I will not allow the people of this country to be intimidated by evil cowards."

———

"Let us let our own children know that we will stand against the forces of fear. When there is talk of hatred, let us stand up and talk against it. When there is talk of violence, let us stand up and talk against it. In the face of death, let us honor life."

———

"We hear too many loud and angry voices in America today whose sole goal seems to be to try to keep some people as paranoid as possible and the rest of us all torn up and upset with each other. They spread hate; they leave the impression, by their very words, that violence is acceptable."

———

From President Clinton's speech at the (one year) memorial service Sunday, April 25, 1996:

"Yesterday, Hillary and I had the privilege of speaking with some children of other federal employees, children like those who were

129

lost here. One little girl said, 'We should all plant a tree in memory of the children.' So this morning before we got on the plane to come here, at the White House, we planted that tree in honor of the children of Oklahoma . . .

"My fellow Americans, a tree takes a long time to grow, and wounds take a long time to heal, but we must begin. Those who are lost now belong to God. Some day we will be with them, but until that happens, their legacy must be our lives."

————

"A year ago I was able to come here and say to you that you have lost too much, but you have not lost everything. You have not lost America. In the year since, America has stood with you and prayed with you and worked with you as you rebuild. But today, I come today to say you have given America something precious—a greater sense of our shared humanity, our common values, our obligations to one another. You've taken some of the meanness out of our national life and put a little more love and respect into it, in ways that you probably cannot even imagine. And I thank you for that."

————

Speech by the president and the first lady to the families of the victims of the Oklahoma City bombing, April 5, 1996:

"Just a few moments ago I was honored to lay a wreath, along with the first lady and some children who survived and their parents, and then to dedicate the child-care center that will be built near the site of the bombing, thanks to the remarkable efforts of your public officials and private citizens together. You have shown how strong you are, and you have given us all an example of the power of faith and community, the power of both God's grace and human courage.

"On this Good Friday, what you have done has demonstrated to a watching and often weary and cynical world that good can overcome evil, that love can outlast hate, that the light of human life can shine on through the most terrible darkness. And so I thank you for that. And I know that you could not have done it without your faith.''

———

"The men, women and children who fell beneath the rubble of the Murrah Federal Building were not cut down in a great battle, they were just ordinary Americans. Simple soldiers of the everyday, going to work, going to play, taking on their responsibilities as parents and providers and citizens.''

———

Plaque Dedication Ceremony for New YMCA Day-Care Center, Oklahoma City, Oklahoma, April 5, 1996:

"But what you have done is to show our children that in the wake of evil, goodness can surround them and lift them up. You have done a lot here already to prove that their lives are strong and powerful— like the tree behind me, which has now become famous around the country. Everybody wants to know why this tree stood up when the bomb went off. It lost its leaves and its bark and it's still kind of ugly—but it survived, and it's going to bloom again.

"Why is it going to bloom again? Because its roots kept it strong and standing.

"The survivors and the spirit of this community are blooming again because your roots kept you strong and standing.''

———

1996 Olympics

"You know, I'm very proud that the United States is going to be hosting the Olympics again and that this is the one hundredth anniversary of the modern games. I'm proud that there will be people from 197 different nations coming here. And when I see these folks behind me, the Olympians and the Paralympians, I know that they will see America at its best.

"They'll see our diversity and our unity; they'll see that we have differences that don't divide us. They'll see that we understand individual excellence and teamwork. They'll see, as Buddy Lee said, that no champion wins alone, not in athletics and not in life. There's always a parent who cares or a teacher who listens or a coach who believes or a friend who encourages or a church and community that supports."

———

"Most of you probably know this, but when the Olympics came back to life in modern times, it was William Milligan Sloan who took it upon himself to organize the first American team. And then when two of his athletes couldn't afford the tickets to Athens, he gave up the tickets that he had. So he never even saw his dream come to life."

———

"Dr. Sloan's first recruit was a man named Robert Garrett, who had never competed in sports before. So he literally started with only a dream, and he had to figure out what he was going to do. He saw a picture of an ancient discus thrower, and he asked a blacksmith to make one for him. Unfortunately, it weighed thirteen pounds. But he didn't know any better. He only knew he could not throw it further than 49 feet.

"He heard the Europeans were throwing it 87 feet, but he showed up for the competition anyway. And when he showed up, the folks took away his thirteen-pound discus and gave him one that weighed two and a half pounds. He tossed it out of the stadium and won the medal. So sometimes our handicaps in life can become great advantages.''

———

Speaking to U.S. Olympic Team, Olympic Village, Atlanta, July 19, 1996:

''I want you to win all the medals you can. I want you to mop up and do great. But I want you to realize that just by being what you already are, you are a source of enormous pride to our country and an inspiration to the world.''

———

''These Olympics are about what's right with America. And Atlanta's magnificent effort at hosting the Olympics is about what's right with America. There are some other things that I believe reflect what's right with America at the Olympics. For example, this year 197 nations have teams, and these teams include places that the United States has helped to move toward peace and freedom. And even in places where the work of peace and freedom is not yet finished, at least there's been enough progress for an Olympic team to emerge.''

———

''All these people in their own way reflect something that's good about America. In many other countries there are athletes who studied and competed and got a good education in the United States. We gave them an opportunity to make the most of their own lives, and now they're giving something back to their native lands. They, too, reflect what's right with America.''

———

"Why do you like the Olympics? I think one reason is—besides the fact that Americans are sports nuts and we all like athletics— I think we like the Olympics because they work the way we think the world ought to work. Everybody shows up, from the smallest island country, which has three or four athletes, to the largest delegation. They all accept the rules of the game; they're all treated with respect; everybody has their chance; everybody gives their best; and even the ones who don't win medals are better off for having tried. And when it's all over, people feel like they were part of something that was bigger than themselves. And that's really how we think the world ought to work."

Thanksgiving

"Thanksgiving is our oldest tradition. In 1789, George Washington made Thanksgiving his first proclamation for our new nation. Much has changed for America in the two centuries since that first proclamation. Today we not only feed ourselves well; our bounty helps to feed the world. The light of freedom that drew founders to our shores not only shines here. For the first time in history, more than half the world's people who once lived in the shadows of tyranny and depression now live under governments of their own choosing.

"On this year's Thanksgiving, we are reminded that we are a nation truly blessed."

Thanksgiving Turkey Ceremony, the Rose Garden, November 27, 1996:

"You all know why we're here. Tomorrow, forty-five million turkeys will pay the supreme sacrifice for our Thanksgiving. So, continuing a tradition begun fifty years ago by President Truman, I am going to keep at least one turkey off of the Thanksgiving dinner table by giving a pardon to a turkey from Ohio that will now go to the petting zoo that Kidwell Farms maintains in Fairfax, Virginia.

"We can all be grateful, therefore, that there will be one less turkey in Washington, D.C., tomorrow."

———

Presidential Politics

POLITICS

Asked why he chose politics:

"It's the only track I ever wanted to run on."

———

"The truth is most politicians are not candid with people. They try to act like they hate politics—and, oh, this is a burden, I just had to do it. When the truth is most of them love it and wouldn't do anything else on a dime if they could avoid it. I'm just more candid than that. I decided when I was a young man that my best use in life would be in public life, that I had some gifts at it and I wanted to make a difference. To me politics is the only area of human life where it's bad form to be ambitious. Nobody criticizes Michael Jordan for the hundreds of free throws he may have shot when he was a kid in North Carolina."

———

"Americans want to hate politics, but they desperately want it to work."

———

To New York radio host Don Imus, May 24, 1993:

"There are always going to be people who want to be president, and some days I'd like to give it to them."

———

"People engaged by their leaders in a conversation feel better about the outcome even if they would prefer a different one, simply because they are given a chance to have their say. Dialogue is the way to teach."

"I came from a family with no money or political influence, particularly. I had a good education. I had a lot of wonderful friends. I was interested in people. I had a chance to work in campaigns and to do other things that gave me a chance to get started. This is a great country that is really open to people of all backgrounds to be successful in public life. But you need to learn, you need to care about people, and then you just need the experience."

Speech to tenth annual convention of the National Association of Hispanic Publications, January 26, 1996:

"Secretary Peña gave me a beautiful introduction, and it illustrates Clinton's first law of politics. Whenever possible, be introduced by someone you have appointed to high office."

Houston DNC Gala, June 21, 1996:

"Let me ask you to think as I leave about this choice and these terms. If you were lucky enough to know right before you leave this earth, the last time you put your head on the pillow that it was your last time, what would you be thinking about? You wouldn't be thinking, I wish I spent more time at the office. And, frankly, you probably wouldn't be thinking, I wish I'd spent more time on politics. You'd be thinking about your children and the people you love and the people you cared about. The things that really mattered in your life. The purpose of politics is simply to give people the space they need to make those memories, and to remind people that you can't really make those memories unless you give other people the same chance and accord them the same respect, even if they're really different from you."

Sioux Falls, South Dakota, November 4, 1996:

"Now, long toward the end of this last Congress they adopted our program. They said, oh, we've got to go face the voters; we'll give the president what he wants. And they hope you have this case of collective amnesia.

"The vice president told a story today in Cleveland when we were together. I had forgotten this story, we used to tell it at home all the time. But it captures what they're trying to get you to think about their budget.

"It's a story about a politician out in the country and he sees a farmer. He's running for office and the farmer is sitting up on his porch rocking and he says, I'm going to go talk to this farmer but there's a big old dog in the yard that's ferocious-looking. So he says, 'Sir, I'd like to come visit with you, but does your dog bite?' He said, 'No.' So he hikes over the fence, goes over on the porch, shakes hands with the farmer and tells him he's running for the legislature and would like to have his vote. And the dog runs up and bites him right in the rear. And he runs back and jumps in his car and rolls the window down and said, 'I thought you said your dog didn't bite.' He said, 'Son that ain't my dog.'

"And let me tell you something, folks, that budget that I ve-toed—it is their dog and it was a mangy old dog, and that's why I vetoed that dog."

———

ABC News This Week *with David Brinkley,* November 10, 1996:
Brinkley: "The voters did not give you a majority of the popular vote and they also chose to keep a Republican House and Senate. Are the people telling us something?"

"I think what they're telling us is they expect us to work together. Whether we like it or not, that's what they want. They want us to run their affairs in Washington the way they try to run their affairs in their homes, in their workplaces, in their civic organizations, in their religious organizations. They want us to reach across the lines that divide.

"I think all these changes that are going on in the world leave people with great ambivalent feelings, but a longing to kind of continue to make progress and preserve their values. And so I think if there was a judgment here it is that if we work together in a sort of a creative tension like we did at the end of this last Congress, we'll get it right and we'll move the country forward."

CONGRESS

Speech to Democrats in Congress, March 30, 1992:

"It ought to be easy for me to avoid being tarred with them, since I have said we need some changes. We need to limit the contribution of [political action committees], to limit the cost of congressional campaigns, to open the airwaves to generate competition, to end pay raises and perks until the pay of ordinary Americans starts to go up again. Part of the problem with Congress is the direct result of not being engaged in the great work of the nation. There is no driving presidential vision which occupies [Congress's] energies. We've turned it into a drab place of contesting interest groups over minor matters because there is no president who says, 'This is the agenda; go get it.' "

"Members of Congress have been defying presidents for a long time."

141

"The trick is, in a funny way, is not to hide the differences, but to get them out in a way that—where those of us on opposite sides can understand the other's opinion. There's a way to make an argument—to get the maximum amount of votes out of it in the shortest amount of time through emotion, and there's a way to make the same argument so that your opponent at least understands your position. And I bet it's the same way here around a gaming table, or anything else. There's two ways to talk to people when you've got a difference of opinion.

"More than half the time in this country—this is an interesting little historical fact—more than half of the presidents who have served have had the Congress in the hands of the opposite party at least one, if not both, houses. Now, that's what—the voters seem to think that's a good idea and they keep doing it. So we have to try to figure out how to make that work."

After having injured his knee in March 1997, he joked that he might pick up a few sympathy votes in Congress:

"I'll take them any way I can get them."

CRITICISM

In 1992 he used a Little Rock fund-raising dinner to lash out at his critics:

"A lot of people criticize me because I get along with people. I thought the object of politics was to get things done. The object of politics in Washington for too long has been to ignore getting anything done but always make sure you're postured right on the evening news."

"I expect criticism. I admit I'm a sinner and have no problem when someone reminds me of that. But I believe we could do better if we talked to one another more and shouted at one another less."

——

DEMOCRATS

"Democrats who want government to do more—and I'm one of them—have to show fiscal responsibility."

——

"I've always been for challenging the Democratic orthodoxy. I've always felt that unless we could become a party seen as pro-growth and pro-environment, pro-civil rights and tough on crime, pro-business as well as pro-labor, we were done as a national party."

——

On the Democratic Party

"I am trying to redefine it, not to run away from the base but to build on the base, to open up the Democratic Party to the majority of people it once represented."

——

"I'm a pro-growth, pro-business and pro-labor, pro-education, pro-health care, pro-environment, pro-family, pro-choice Democrat."

——

REPUBLICANS

From a speech in heavily Republican Orange County, California,
November 2, 1992:

"I want you to go out in the next twelve days to talk to your
friends and neighbors and tell them it won't kill them if they hold
their noses and vote for a Democrat one time, because they'll like
what they get."

1992 campaign:

"A Clinton administration won't spend your money on programs
that don't solve problems and a government that doesn't work."

---

*1993: Presenting a birthday cake to House GOP Leader Bob Michel,
seventy, at lunch with Capitol Hill Republicans:*

"I realize this is against my best interests, but I want to invite you
to make a wish."

---

*1996: Asked if he would have Republicans in his Cabinet if
reelected:*

"Well, let me say I certainly wouldn't rule it out. You know, I
very much like to operate in a bipartisan fashion. I like to get
people together and work together and practice principled
compromise."

PARTISANSHIP

"The most important thing is that this United States of America needs at least one political party that's not afraid to tell the people the truth and address the real needs of human beings. We're not here to save the Democratic Party, we're here to save the United States of America . . . For more than a decade, we have lived in a fantasy world in which it was bad form and terrible politics to admit that we had problems of this magnitude . . . The Republican burden is their record of denial, evasion, and neglect. But our burden is to give the people a new choice rooted in old values . . . We've got to have a message that touches everybody, that makes sense to everybody, that goes beyond the stale orthodoxies of 'left' and 'right.' "

———

State of the Union Address, February 5, 1997:

"We must work together. The people of this nation elected us all. They want us to be partners, not partisans. They put us all right here in the same boat, they gave us all oars and they told us to row."

———

"The lesson of our history is clear: When we put aside partisanship, embrace the best ideas regardless of where they come from, and work for principled compromise, we can move America not left or right, but forward. That is what I am determined to do."

———

"You also know that I have done my best to reach across party lines to work with Republicans of good will; that I think this intense partisanship—the idea that everybody who is not in your

145

party is the enemy of your future and the enemy of your country—is crazy; the idea that you should never work with people even if you agree with them on a specific issue because there might be some, God forbid, benefit to somebody in the other party is wrong. That is not what made America great. There are enough differences that are honest without that kind of accepted partisanship."

———

Democratic National Dinner, Coral Gables, Florida, April 29, 1996:

"There's a lot of talk about the word 'empowerment.' And I used it a lot in 1992, and long before I decided to run for president. I believe in it. To use the words of my friend, James Carville, and Larry Hawkins said, 'Everybody in America ought to read James Carville's book, *We're Right and They're Wrong.*' So I'll flack for it tonight. But Carville said, you know, people criticize the Democrats for giving people fish when we ought to be teaching them to fish, but our opponents want to drain the pond."

———

Second Inaugural Address, January 20, 1997:

"The American people returned to office a president of one party and a Congress of another. Surely they did not do this to advance the politics of petty bickering and extreme partisanship they plainly deplore. No, they call all of us instead to be repairers of the breach and to move on with America's mission. America demands and deserves big things from us, and nothing big ever came from being small."

———

THE PRESS

"They [reporters] should do their watchdog function, but anyone who lets himself be interpreted to the American people through these intermediaries alone is nuts."

To a press conference:

"You know why I can stiff you on the press conferences? Because Larry King liberated me by giving me to the American people directly."

Shortly after taking office, Clinton had lunch with Arthur Ochs Sulzberger, Jr., publisher of The New York Times. *Asked if Clinton had a friend at the* Times, *Sulzberger told him "The best way of describing our relationship with you is 'tough love.' " Laughing, Clinton returned:*

"Well, just don't forget the love part."

Speech to Mayor's Youth Council, Boston, Massachusetts, January 31, 1995:
"Mr. President, I notice that often it's the media that is responsible for the negative portrayal of young people in our society. And I realize that we need strong leadership to help convince the media that it is—that there is a lot good news about today's youth. How can you help us get that message across?"

"I don't know that I'm the best one to ask about negative portrayals."

What's the best advice you've gotten as president about being president?

"Never pick a fight with people who buy ink by the barrel."

Speech to White House Correspondents' Dinner, May 4, 1996:

"So, if we can all agree on the ground rules—I'd like to give you a sense of the musings of my inner candidate. You can attribute these remarks to a source inside the president's suit.

"Now, I had occasion to give this topic considerable thought last weekend as I was going through the Sunday classified ads. Gosh, there must have been eight and a half million listings—all of them at good wages. But I couldn't find a single job I'd prefer to this one."

PUBLIC LIFE

"I remember very clearly. I was a junior in high school and had been interested in being a physician and a musician and a couple of other things, but I just made a decision that I would try to go into public service because I thought I'd be good at it and I thought it would be interesting. I thought I'd never have to worry about getting up and going to work every day because it would always be different. I was interested in people and human nature."

"We also live in a time when people think pretty poorly about anybody who is in public life."

"You know, when I started out in public life with a lot of my friends from the Arkansas delegation down here— there used to be a saying from time to time that every man who runs for public office will claim that he was born in a log cabin he built with his

148

own hands. Well, my mother knew better. And she made sure I did, too. Long before she even met Hillary, my mother knew it takes a village, and she was grateful for the support she got.

"I believe that one of the things that breeds cynicism in public life is when there seems to be a gross difference between the image and the reality."

———

"My faith has taught me to see this as a ministry. I think everybody has work to do, and you're supposed to do the best you can . . . every person has a calling in life, and you should try to make the most of your work. Each person can fulfill the intention of God for human life by giving dignity to whatever work they do."

———

Historical
Perspectives

"Look, the genius of democracy, the thing the Founding Fathers understood, was that by definition most people who could ever get elected to anything could do most of what they'd have to do. To be preoccupied with the institution of the presidency keeps you from thinking about the people who sent you there and the problems they have. I really do get up every day and just put one foot in front of the other and not think about 'it' as if it were some disembodied thing. I'm just going to do the very best I can and try to have a wonderful time doing it."

———

"From our revolution to the Civil War, to the Great Depression to the civil-rights movement, our people have always mustered the determination to construct from these crises the pillars of our history."

———

Two hundredth Birthday Celebration of Youngstown, Ohio, and one hundred and fiftieth Birthday Celebration of Mahoning County, Ohio, July 4, 1996:

"Two centuries ago at another time of great challenge and change, a group of Revolutionary War veterans were given this piece of land in an unchartered wilderness. They were told to go take the land, cut the path to the west and to the American future, take responsibility to seize the opportunities offered by our young democracy. They were pathfinders into a new land—trailblazers for our new nation. Their work helped to build us into the greatest, strongest, most prosperous nation in the world."

———

"This room is a good reminder of why teams and why this country should never say die. And I think I should tell you this. It was in this room in 1814, 182 years ago, that symbolically the light of liberty in America almost went out. This room was all set up for a fancy banquet, and unbeknownst to the people who were planning to come, in the War of 1812, the British had actually landed a few miles from here.

"And our President, James Madison, was the last president of the United States that actually was the operating commander in chief of the Armed Forces. He was out of the White House, and his wife, Dolley, was basically going to host this dinner they were having. And so James Madison sent his wife word that the British were coming and that she should get out of here before she was killed.

"But she had to save that picture of George Washington, which was painted in 1797, two hundred years ago next year, by Gilbert Stuart. And we bought it for $500 in 1797. It's worth a dollar or two more today. She cut that picture out of a frame, rolled it up, and just before the British rolled in here she cleared out, along with all the partygoers.

"They came in and had the gall to eat all of our food, and then they burned the house down. And a lot of people thought the next day that America's days were numbered. It didn't turn out that way.

"And I think if we all remember that we can do more in our own lives to help our country, our team, our families and our communities. And that's the sort of spirit you have exhibited. I hope you'll—when times get tough, you'll remember that story. That was a long time ago, and we're still here."

National African-American History Month, February 22, 1993:

"Understanding our past makes us aware of how far we have come and how far we have to go. Last month, for the first time in many years, our National Archives displayed for the public the Emancipation Proclamation. That document, signed by President Abraham Lincoln on January 1, 1863, launched the beginning of a life of freedom for millions of African-American people.

"For several months last year, individuals and groups of citizens had been writing to the National Archives to inquire whether the historic document would be exhibited over the New Year holiday in honor of its anniversary. After considering the matter, the National Archives decided to arrange an exhibit.

"The fragile document was shown in our Nation's Capital for five days adjacent to the original Charters of Freedom—the Declaration of Independence, the Constitution of the United States, and the Bill of Rights. The exhibit reminded America of how liberty had once been denied to a particular segment of our population. The diverse backgrounds of the people in those lines each day, however, showed how the history of African-Americans touches all of us."

———

Address at centennial celebration, American University, Washington, D.C., February 26, 1993:

"Twice before in this century, history has asked the United States and other great powers to provide leadership for a world ravaged by war. After World War I, that call went unheeded. . . . And the result was instability, inflation, then depression, and, ultimately, a Second World War.

"After the second war, we refused to let history repeat itself. Led by a great American president, Harry Truman, a man of very common roots but uncommon vision, we drew together with other Western powers to reshape a new era."

———

"There could be no better place for this discussion than the National Archives, for within these walls are America's bedrocks of our common ground—the Declaration of Independence, the Constitution, the Bill of Rights. No paper is as lasting as the words these documents contain. So we put them in these special cases to protect the parchment from the elements. No building is as solid as the principles these documents embody, but we sure tried to build one with these metal doors eleven inches thick to keep them safe, for these documents are America's only crown jewels. But the best place of all to hold these words and these principles is the one place in which they can never fade and never grow old—in the stronger chambers of our hearts."

———

Speech at welcome home rally, the White House, November 6, 1996:

"And just for your information, George Clinton of New York, doubtless a relative of mine—the only man in America ever to be the governor of a state in excess of twenty years. He served for twenty-one years as governor of New York. He served four years and then laid out and served seventeen years, until he became vice president. And that's a pretty good record. It just sort of runs in the family, you know."

———

From a speech at Georgetown, 1992:

"More than two hundred years ago, our founders outlined our first social compact between government and the people not just between lords and kings. More than a century ago, Abraham Lincoln gave his life to maintain the union that compact created. Sixty years ago, Franklin Roosevelt renewed that promise with a New Deal that offered opportunity in return for hard work.

155

"Today we need to forge a New Covenant that will repair the damaged bond between the people and their government and restore our basic values—the notion that our country has a responsibility to help people get ahead. That citizens have not only the right but a responsibility to rise as far and as high as their talents and determination can take them, and that we're all in this together. We must make good on the words of Thomas Jefferson, who said, 'A debt of service is due from every man to his country proportional to the bounties which nature and fortune have measured him.'

"Make no mistake: This New covenant means change—change in our party, change in our national leadership, and change in our country. Far away from Washington, in your hometowns and mine, people have lost faith in the ability of government to change their lives for the better: Out there, you can hear the quiet, troubled voice of the forgotten middle class, lamenting that government no longer looks out for their interests or honors their values . . ."

————

On his own place in history:

"I would like to be remembered for leading America's transition into the twenty-first century, in a period of sweeping change at home in how we work and live and relate to each other, a period of sweeping changes in the world."

————

AMERICA

Oval Office, November 27, 1995:

"From our birth, America has always been more than just a place. America has embodied an idea that has become the ideal for billions of people throughout the world. Our founders said it best: America is about life, liberty, and the pursuit of happiness.

"In this century especially, America has done more than simply stand for these ideals. We have acted on them and sacrificed for them. Our people fought two world wars so that freedom could triumph over tyranny. After World War I, we pulled back from the world, leaving a vacuum that was filled by the forces of hatred. After World War II, we continued to lead the world. We made the commitments that kept the peace, that helped to spread democracy, that created unparalleled prosperity, and that brought victory in the Cold War."

———

Second Inaugural Address, January 20, 1997:

"The promise of America was born in the eighteenth century out of the bold conviction that we are all created equal. It was extended and preserved in the nineteenth century, when our nation spread across the continent, saved the Union and abolished the scourge of slavery.

"Then in turmoil and triumph, that promise exploded onto the world stage to make this the American century."

———

"This is America. There is no 'them.' There's only us."

———

"This is a country founded on a certain set of ideas, a certain set of values, a certain set of principles. And anybody willing to embrace them, to work hard to make the most of their own lives, to be responsible, can be an American citizen. That is the special thing about the United States and we should never forget it."

———

"Americans have ever been a restless, questing, hopeful people. We must bring to our task today the vision and will of those who came before us . . . Let us begin with energy and hope, with faith and discipline, and let us work until our work is done.''

―――

"The America of our ideals is one where every child can wish to become an astronaut, a doctor, a teacher, a general or a business owner—because there are role models and positive avenues of opportunity for all our children.''

―――

"Our democracy must be not only the envy of the world but the engine of our own renewal. There is nothing wrong with America that cannot be cured by what is right with America.''

―――

December 15, 1994:

"With all of our problems, this is still the greatest country in the world—standing not at the twilight, but at the dawn of our greatest days. We still have a lot to be thankful for. Let's all remember that.''

―――

"Our ability to re-create ourselves at critical junctures is why we're still around after all this time.''

―――

State of the Union Address, January 25, 1994:

"When the earth shook and fires raged in California, when I saw the Mississippi deluge the farmlands of the Midwest in a five-hundred-year flood, when the century's bitterest cold swept from

North Dakota to Newport News, it seemed as though the world itself was coming apart at the seams. But the American people— they just came together. They rose to the occasion, neighbor helping neighbor, strangers risking life and limb to save total strangers—showing the better angels of our nature.

"Let us not reserve the better angels only for natural disasters, leaving our deepest and most profound problems to petty political fighting. Let us instead be true to our spirit—facing facts, coming together, bringing hope and moving forward."

THE AMERICAN DREAM

"We must return to the principle that if we give ordinary people equal opportunity, quality education, and a fair shot at the American dream, they will do extraordinary things."

"This country works best when it works together. For decades after World War II, we gave more and more Americans a chance to live out their dreams. I know—I'm blessed to be one of them. I was born to a widowed mother at a time when my state's income was barely half the national average; the first person in my family to finish college, thanks to money my parents couldn't really afford—scholarships, loans, and a half a dozen jobs. It breaks my heart to see people with their own dreams for themselves and their children shattered. And I'm going to do all I can to turn it around. But I need your help. We can do it."

"There are three things I want for America. I want the American dream to be alive for every single man and woman and boy and

159

girl who is willing to work for it, no matter what their race, their background, their income, their gender, their condition of disability.

"I want this country to continue to be the light of the world and the leader of the world for peace and freedom and security and prosperity, in a new era in which the Cold War is fading away, but we still have to deal with things like terrorism and ethnic, religious and racial hatreds crossing national lines, the proliferation of weapons, the proliferation of drug dealing and organized crime. This country needs to be fighting that fight around the world to keep it better here at home for our people.

"And finally, as you look around this crowd today and you see a picture of America, I want our country to go into the next century strengthened by our diversity, not weakened by it. I want us to be coming together, not drifting apart."

———

Prior Presidents

"The American presidents who have prevailed over the long run . . . did it because the people were with them, and the other people who worked with them knew it."

———

"If you read history books as president, you begin to put yourself in the position of the person at the time. And you realize that a lot of the kinds of dilemmas are similar. So you learn things about the importance of finding your voice and how words are more important than you ever imagined them to be."

———

Asked about planning his 1992 Inaugural Address:

"I'm gonna go back and read a number of the other speeches. I want to read Andrew Jackson's Inaugural speech, the first one. I think Lincoln's Second Inaugural was one of his greatest speeches. He did the best job of capturing huge ideas and transient events in a few words and crystallizing what was going to happen.''

———

"If you think about our most successful periods of reform, these initiatives have been shaped by presidents who incorporated what was good, smoothed out what was rough and discarded what would hurt. That was the role of Theodore Roosevelt and Woodrow Wilson in the aftermath of the populist era. That was the role of Franklin Roosevelt in the aftermath of the La Follette progressive movement. And that is my job in the next hundred days and for all the days I serve as president.''

———

The (John) Adams Family

At unveiling of Bush portrait, the East Room, July 17, 1995:

"Many of you know that it was in this room that Abigail Adams used to dry the family laundry when the room was nothing more than a brick shell. You may not know that the great explorer, Meriwether Lewis, set up camp here, surrounded by canvas tarps, books, and hunting rifles in the day when he was Thomas Jefferson's secretary. John Quincy Adams frequently would come here to watch the sun rise after he finished his early-morning swim in the Potomac. That also is something we're considering taking up if the heat wave doesn't break.''

———

Thomas Jefferson

"Thomas Jefferson believed that to preserve the very foundations of our nation, we would need dramatic change from time to time. Well, my fellow Americans, this is our time. Let us embrace it.''

Abraham Lincoln

"I have always been, from childhood, captivated by the figure of Lincoln, not only the historic significance of what he did but what kind of person he was and how he was able, under enormous pressure and frequent ridicule, to hold on to the simple idea that the Union had to be preserved, and then how he was able to move the country to the point where he could break his most famous campaign promise, which was not to free the slaves, and instead issue the Emancipation Proclamation."

"Lincoln has always been an inspiration to me because he overcame personal difficulties and public humiliations, because he had vision and conviction, and he was willing to be misunderstood until he could complete his life's work. He had this incredibly complex personality and very fertile mind, but he knew he had to focus people's attention and his own will on saving the Union. I basically think that's what has to happen now in revitalizing and reuniting this country."

". . . as President Lincoln once so powerfully reminded us, this country cannot afford to be materially rich and spiritually poor."

Theodore Roosevelt

"Here's what I believe. I think Teddy Roosevelt, our first great environmental president, and a Republican, was right. I believe that we cannot preserve the American economy unless we have a system for sustaining our natural resources—our land, our air, our water, our trees, our species. That's what I believe.''

———

"Remember, it was a great Republican president, Theodore Roosevelt, who set our nation on the path of conservation. In 1908, he said, 'Any right-thinking parent earnestly desires and strives to leave a child both an untarnished name and a reasonable equipment for the struggle of life.' So this nation as a whole should earnestly desire and struggle to leave to the next generation the national honor unstained and the national resources unexhausted. It sounded good in 1908, and it's even more important as we stand on the edge of a new century.''

———

Woodrow Wilson

"When you read the biographies of these guys—I'm almost done with August Heckscher's biography of Woodrow Wilson, which is an interesting book that a friend of mine sent me—you realize that the success of a president, in part, is going to depend on the time that they're in. And some of our failed presidents, had they been president at a different time, might have actually been quite good. And some of our greatest presidents were great just for the moment at which they lived. Had they served at a different time, they might have fallen in another category.''

———

Franklin Delano Roosevelt

1980 Democratic Convention, referring to FDR in 1936:
"We were still in the teeth of the Depression. Why was he returned to office? Because people knew what sort of vision he had for

163

America. They knew what action he was taking to transform the country. And they were willing, most important, to accept hardship for the present, because they believed they were part of a process that would lead them to a better tomorrow.

"[Roosevelt] . . . didn't get this country off its back by saying 'The only thing we have to fear is a lack of venture capital.' "

———

Harry S Truman

Asked whether he looked to Truman for inspiration:

"Yes. Because I'm from Arkansas and Truman was from Missouri, and because a lot of the political people of my youth were big Truman supporters—you know our state voted for him in 1948, when a lot of the South abandoned him—I've always had an awareness of Truman's legacy. And he's always been one of my four or five favorite presidents."

———

"Who is the last president, while sitting in office, who took on the National Rifle Association? Who is the last person who took on the array of health-care interests, who could spend $200 million or $300 million to perform reverse plastic surgery on the president and the first lady? I tell you who it was; Harry Truman. With, I might add, the same result, in terms of standing in the polls. Harry Truman was just like me, in the sense he was a middle-class guy who cared about middle-class people. Except he got down to about twenty-seven percent in the polls. All I'm saying is I think you can tell if a person has convictions by the fights they fight, the battles they undertake. This idea that there's some battle for my soul is the biggest bunch of hooey I ever saw. I know who I am; I know what I believe."

John F. Kennedy

The night he won the nomination, 1992, referring to JFK:

"The rules of the convention preclude my acceptance tonight, but thirty-two years ago, another young candidate who wanted to get this country moving again came to the convention to say a small 'thank-you.' "

Asked about JFK and the revelations about his personal life:

"I think I have a . . . much different perspective of him now than I did when I was seventeen or sixteen. He . . . inspired a whole generation of young people to believe that public service was an honorable good thing, that America was a great country and that we could make it better and that was very important. You know, if you look at the whole history of the American—many presidents have had different kinds of personal problems. I wonder if Abraham Lincoln could get elected today if it were known how severe his depressions were before he took office, but I'm awful glad he got elected. He probably was our greatest president, certainly in some ways he was our greatest president."

Lyndon Johnson

"You know, I feel bad about Johnson, I admire him so much and in so many ways, and I think that if he could have been president at a slightly different time, he might have done so well . . .

"Johnson was remarkable, though. He had a way of talking and dealing with people that was just fascinating. He got a lot done."

Richard M. Nixon

Statement upon the death of former President Nixon, April 22, 1994:

"It's impossible to be in this job without feeling a special bond with the people who have gone before, and I was deeply grateful to President Nixon for his wise counsel on so many occasions on many issues over the last year. His service to me and to our country during this period was like the rest of his service to the nation for nearly a half century—he gave of himself with intelligence and devotion to duty. And his country owes him a debt of gratitude for that service."

Jimmy Carter

Asked what will happen when he leaves office:

"I have thought some about the life of ex-presidents. I think it is possible that President Jimmy Carter will have the most enduring impact of any former president, partly because he set up a system and a structure and a support mechanism for his activities, partly because they are so wide-ranging, and partly because he is so energetic and imaginative."

Ronald Reagan

"Substantively, the best thing he did early was to restore the country's sense of confidence and optimism and possibility."

George Bush

At unveiling of Bush portrait, the East Room, July 17, 1995:

"It's impossible to live in this wonderful old place without becoming incredibly attached to it—to the history of our country and to what each and every one of these rooms represent. In a way, I think every family who has ever lived here has become more and more a part of our country's history, just for the privilege of sleeping under this roof at night. And so, perhaps the most important thing I can say to President and Mrs. Bush today is, welcome home. We're glad to have you back."

———

"As Americans look for ways to come together to deal with the challenges we face today, they can do well in looking at the lives of President and Mrs. Bush. They have been guided by the basic American values and virtues of honesty, compassion, civility, responsibility, and optimism. They have passed these values on to their family and on to our American family as well. And for that we should all be profoundly grateful."

———

Foreign Policy

"The dividing line between foreign and domestic policy is increasingly blurred. Our administration will be forced to spend a lot of time on foreign policy whether we want to or not."

"The U.S. should use its diplomatic and economic leverage to increase the material incentives to democratize and raise the costs for those who will not. We have every right to condition our foreign aid and debt-relief policies on demonstrable progress toward democracy and market reforms."

"Promoting democracy around the world we must reinforce the powerful global movement toward democracy. U.S. foreign policy cannot be divorced from the moral principles that most Americans share. We cannot disregard the manner in which other governments treat their own people, whether their domestic institutions are democratic or repressive or whether they help encourage or check illegal conduct beyond their borders. Recent experience from Panama, to Iran, to Iraq, shows the danger of forging strategic relationships with despotic regimes.

"It should matter to us how others govern themselves. Democracies do not go to war with each other. The French and British have nuclear weapons, but we do not fear annihilation at their hands. Democracies don't sponsor terrorist acts against each other. They are more likely to be reliable trading partners, protect the global environment, and abide by international law. Over time, democracy is a stabilizing force. It provides nonviolent means for resolving disputes. Democracies do a better job of protecting ethnic, religious, and other minorities, and elections can help resolve fratricidal civil wars.

"An American foreign policy of engagement for democracy will unite our interests and values."

"Ethnic cleansing in the former Yugoslavia is but the most brutal and blatant and ever-present manifestation of what we see also with the opposition of the Kurds in Iraq, the abusive treatment of the Baha'i in Iran, the endless race-based violence in South Africa. And in many other places we are reminded again and again how fragile are the safeguards of civilization."

———

"Now I understand why presidents get so captivated by foreign policy. It's fun. Now we've got to get back to work."

———

"No American foreign policy can succeed if it slights our commitment to democracy."

———

"You get such wonderful warm receptions in places like Northern Ireland. Why won't people cut you a break back here?"

"Oh, but that's as old as time. In the Bible it says a prophet is not without honor except in his own home. So that's probably endemic to human nature. But when I go abroad, also, I represent the United States, so it's not just me. The end of the Cold War has left us as not only the world's only superpower but a genuinely trusted country. Most people believe we have no ulterior motives, that we don't want anything out of Bosnia, we don't want anything out of the Middle East, we don't want anything out of Northern Ireland—except that our people would be more secure if we lived in a more peaceful world."

"And I see that so clearly as I travel around the world. I see that Americans are still looked up to by people around the world who think that we don't want to control their lives and we want to use our power to help everybody live in peace, who think that we are struggling to find ways for all of our folks to live together instead of defining our lives by who we're against and who we're not."

"If we do maintain our partnerships and our leadership, we need not act alone. As we saw in the Gulf War and in Haiti, many other nations who share our goals will also share our burdens. But when America does not lead, the consequences can be very grave, not only for others, but eventually for us as well."

"I know that either I or my successors will make some mistakes in our judgments about what the United States should do around the world. But basically, it is right for us to continue to reach out to other countries. It is right for us to support peace and freedom and to try to expand our own prosperity by expanding that of others.

"It is right for us to be partners with other countries, even when we're tired and we want to lay our burdens down, because it's the only way to fight terrorism, the only way to fight drug-dealing, the only way to fight organized crime; it is right to do that.''

———

Bosnia
1992

"Anything we can do to try to turn up the heat and reduce the carnage is worth trying."

———

"The United States and the international community must take action. If the horrors of the Holocaust taught us anything, it is the high cost of remaining silent and paralyzed in the face of genocide. We must discover who is responsible and take steps to bring them to justice for these crimes against humanity."

———

1993

"If you look at the turmoil all through the Balkans, if you look at the other places where this could play itself out in other parts of the world, this is not just about Bosnia. On the other hand, there is reason to be humble when approaching anything dealing with the former Yugoslavia."

———

"I do not think we should act alone; nor do I think we will have to."

———

"History has shown that you can't allow the mass extermination of people and just sit by and watch it happen."

"The U.S. will not act alone in Bosnia. America is ready to do its part. But Europe must be willing to act with us. We must go forward together."

1995

"The war of ethnic and religious hatred in Bosnia strikes at the heart of our ideal. It's the sort of thing that led to hatred in the hearts of people in the Middle East and cost Prime Minister Rabin his life. It's the sort of thing that cost Abraham Lincoln his life. We have to—we have to—stand against this.

"It's convenient now to forget, but there was a time when Bosnia, too, found unity in its diversity; when Sarajevo was one of the most beautiful and peaceful, multiethnic cities in all of Europe. It can happen again if we stand up for our principles and stand up for our interests; if we are willing to be leaders for peace."

"My fellow Americans, in this new era there are still times when America and America alone can and should make the difference for peace.

"The terrible war in Bosnia is such a case. Nowhere today is the need for American leadership more stark or more immediate than in Bosnia."

1996 speech to the 1st Armored Division, army base in Baum-holder, Germany:

"For three years, I refused to send our American forces into Bosnia where they could have been pulled into war. But I do want you to go there on a mission of peace."

"They need that help because after nearly four years of terrible brutality, trust is in short supply in Bosnia, and they will trust you to do the job right."

CHINA

To Foreign Policy Association, New York, New York, April 1, 1992:

"In China, the president continues to coddle aging rulers with undisguised contempt for democracy, human rights, and the need to control the spread of dangerous technologies. Such forbearance on our part might have been justified during the Cold War as a strategic necessity, when China was a counterweight to Soviet power. But it makes no sense to play the China card now, when our opponents have thrown in their hand."

"We want China to be a successful country . . . a leading country. We are not trying to contain it in any sense."

CUBA

"Let me be clear. The Cuban government will not succeed in any attempt to dictate American immigration policy."

———

"The real problem is the stubborn refusal of the Castro regime to have an open democracy and an open economy, and I think the policies we are following will hasten the day when that occurs."

———

Hartford debate, October 6, 1996:

"For the last four years we have worked hard to put more and more pressure on the Castro government to bring about more openness and a move toward democracy. In 1992, before I became president, Congress passed the Cuba Democracy Act, and I enforced it vigorously. We made the embargo tougher, but we increased contacts, people to people, with the Cubans, including direct telephone service, which are largely supported by the Cuban American community."

———

"Every single country in Latin America, Central America, and the Caribbean is a democracy tonight but Cuba. And if we stay firm and strong, we will be able to bring Cuba around as well."

———

EUROPE

"Thirty-one years ago, President Kennedy made a statement that I believe holds as true today as it did then. He said, 'We see in Europe a partner with whom we could deal on the basis of full equality.' "

"As NATO expands, so will security for all Europe . . . no country outside will be allowed to veto expansion."

———

". . . drawing a new line across Europe . . . could create a self-fulfilling prophecy of future confrontation."

———

"We need to sort of gin up the collective spirit of Europe."

———

GERMANY

With Chancellor Kohl in Milwaukee, May 23, 1996:

". . . it is important that every American know that if you look ahead at the opportunities the world will bring us, we cannot seize those opportunities alone. If we want to trade with other nations, it takes two to tango. Germany and the United States are the greatest trading nations in the world, and we have to lead the fight for fair and free trade."

———

In Berlin, July 12, 1994:

"You have proved that no wall can forever contain the mighty power of freedom."

———

HAITI

"Nearly two hundred years ago, the Haitian people rose up out of slavery and declared their independence. Unfortunately, the promise of liberty was quickly snuffed out.

"And ever since, Haiti has known more suffering and repression than freedom.

"In our time, as democracy has spread throughout our hemisphere, Haiti has been left behind."

———

"The message of the United States to the Haitian dictators is clear: your time is up."

———

"Now the United States must protect its interest: to stop the brutal atrocities that threaten tens of thousands of Haitians; to secure our borders and preserve stability in our hemisphere; to promote democracy and uphold the reliability of our commitment around the world."

———

"I want this to be a country which, twenty years from now, thirty years from now, is still the strongest force in the world for peace and freedom and democracy and prosperity. And that means for me I've had to take some fairly unpopular decisions to keep that possibility alive. Not many people thought it was right to go into Haiti, but we don't have all those refugees at our shore, and they've got freedom now. And I'm proud that we did it, and I'm proud of our people who did it."

IRAQ

In response to reports that Iraqi troops were moving toward Kuwait in 1994:

"Let us watch this with concern, but let us not blow it out of proportion. Let's just deal with the facts as they unfold. But it would be a grave mistake for Saddam Hussein to believe that for any reason the United States would have weakened its resolve on the same issues that involved us in the conflict just a few years ago."

IRELAND

During a 1995 trip he stopped in Dublin at Cassidy's Pub:

"My mother was a Cassidy. All these people came who had been identified as our relatives, and we sat and laughed and talked."

St. Patrick's Day Celebration, 1996:

"We all know that we come tonight in a celebration that is not as unambiguous as we might have hoped . . . Tonight, in the land of our ancestors, the future once again is at a crossroads. And, once again, each of us must do our part to safeguard the promise, the precious promise of peace."

"The truth is no one knows whether human nature craves dominance and division over peace and hope, but we all believe we know, and in the believing we can make a new reality . . . If we believe we are children of God, then what is important is what we are, not what we are not. And that is the gift that Irish-Americans must give Ireland in our lifetime.''

Northern Ireland

Speech during visit to Northern Ireland in 1995:

"To all of you who asked me to do what I could to help peace take root, I pledge you America's support. We will stand with you as you take risks for peace."

Women's Leadership Forum, July 17, 1996:

"Hillary and I went to Northern Ireland in December and they were the happiest people you ever saw. People—the Catholics and the Protestants—cheering, six, seven deep in the street, happy. They couldn't even remember what they were fighting about. A few irresponsible people slip the tracks, doesn't take any time, the people are fighting again. Defining their lives in terms of what religion they're not, which side of the street they don't live on, who they aren't, who they could look down on, who they can march against or throw a rock against. It's wrong and it's foolish and it's self-defeating, but it's so easy."

Israel

1992 campaign:

"Israel should never be grateful to the U.S. for defending it in the Gulf War. The U.S. should be grateful to Israel for its forbearance of the Gulf War."

"Peace that does not provide for Israel's security will not itself be a secure and lasting peace."

October 1994:

"Here in the great Rift Valley you have bridged the tragic rift that separated your people for too long. Here in this region, which is the home of not only both your faiths, but mine, I say: 'Blessed are the peacemakers, for they shall inherit the earth.' "

American-Israel Public Affairs Committee Policy Conference, April 28, 1996:

"When the prime minister said that Israel was now spending as much money on education as defense, I thought of seeing if I could get him to stay another week and just testify before a few committees."

"Our commitment to Israel's security is unshakable. It will stay that way because Israel must have the means to defend itself by itself. In a time of shrinking resources, we have maintained our economic assistance. We have sought to enhance Israel's security, to lessen the risks it has taken and still takes every day for peace."

JAPAN

At Tokyo Summit, July 1993:

"In hard times we shouldn't react like porcupines. We should open up like sunflowers."

———

After breaking off trade negotiations with the Japanese in 1994:

"It is better to have reached no agreement than to have reached an empty agreement."

———

"In Tokyo today a consumer can drive to work in a Chrysler Jeep, talk with a friend on a Motorola telephone, snack on an apple from Washington state, and have American rice for dinner. Of course, a Japanese speaker could say the same thing about an American using all Japanese products, and it's nice now that both of us can tell that story. Of course, our work is not done. We must achieve further progress. But we are making a real difference for American exports and jobs."

———

THE MIDDLE EAST

1992 campaign:

"We must remember that even if the Arab-Israeli dispute were resolved tomorrow, there would still be ample causes of conflict in the Middle East: ancient tribal, ethnic, and religious hatreds; control of oil and water; the bitterness of the have-nots toward those who have; the lack of democratic institutions to hold leaders accountable to their people and restrain their actions abroad; and the territorial ambitions of Iraq and Syria. We have paid a terrible price for the administration's earlier policies of deference to Saddam Hussein. Today, we must deal with Hafez Assad in Syria, but we must not overlook his tyrannical rule and domination of Lebanon."

"As we promote peace in the Middle East . . . so should we also promote democracy in the Middle East."

1993:

"We cannot impose a solution in the Middle East. Only the leaders of the region can make peace. Theirs is an awesome responsibility. Those who oppose the process, who seek to subvert it through violence and intimidation, will find no tolerance here for their methods. But those who are willing to make peace will find in me and my administration a full partner. This is a historic moment. It can slip away all too easily. But if we seize the opportunity, we can begin now to construct a peaceful Middle East for future generations."

1994:
On signing of peace between Israel and Jordan, King Hussein and Yitzhak Rabin:

"Our goal must be to spread prosperity and security to all. [It is] a fundamental law of humanity that what we have in common is more important than our differences."

"In the eighteen years since Egypt and Israel made a miracle at Camp David, Israelis and Arabs have changed the course of history in their lands. Step by step, courageously they have broken with the past, laying down the arms of war and opening their arms to one another. But with every milestone passed along the road of peace and progress the enemies of peace have grown more desperate and more depraved. They know they cannot compete in the marketplace of ideas, they know they have nothing to offer but hardship and despair. And so they resort to murderous attacks that are an affront to the civilized world, and to the moral precepts that lie at the core of the three faiths represented here."

Democratic National Committee Dinner, St. Louis, September 10, 1996:

"I saw the prime minister of Israel yesterday, and we practically had a celebration because he spoke with Mr. Arafat. But the truth is the Palestinians and the Israelis need each other. And if they were getting along, there would be no end to the good they could do for themselves and for their children and the future in the Middle East."

RUSSIA

During 1991 trip to Europe and the Soviet Union:

"People in the Soviet Union crave the type of democracy we take for granted. It was absolutely fascinating to see them embracing what we take for granted."

Speech to Foreign Policy Association, New York, April 1, 1992:

"We need to respond forcefully to one of the greatest security challenges of our time, to help the people of the former Soviet bloc demilitarize their societies and build free political and economic institutions. We have a chance to engage the Russian people in the West for the first time in their history.

"The stakes are high. The collapse of communism is not an isolated event; it's part of a worldwide march toward democracy whose outcome will shape the next century. For ourselves and for millions of people who seek to live in freedom and prosperity, this revolution must not fail."

———

Moscow State University, Russia, April 10, 1995:

"Your decision for democracy and cooperation has given us the opportunity to work together to fulfill the promise of our common victory over forces of fascism fifty years ago. I know that it was not an easy decision to make, and that it is not always an easy decision to stay with. I know what you in Russia will have to do to chart your own democratic course based on your own tradition and culture, as well as on the common challenges we face."

———

Moscow State University, Russia, April 10, 1995:

"The United States supports the forces of democracy and reform here in Russia, because it is in our national interest to do so. I have worked hard to make this post–Cold War world a safer and more hopeful place for the American people. As president, that is my job. That is every president's job. But I have had the opportunity, unlike my recent predecessors, to work with Russia instead of being in opposition to Russia. And I want to keep it that way."

Address to Democratic National Convention, August 26, 1996:

"Nothing in our lifetimes has been more heartening than when people of the former Soviet Union and Central Europe broke the grip of communism. We have aided their progress and I am proud of it. And I will continue our strong partnership with a democratic Russia. And we will bring some of Central Europe's new democracies into NATO, so that they will never question their own freedom in the future."

———

VIETNAM

Asked during 1992 campaign if he wished he'd gone to Vietnam:

"I can't say that. You know, I was raised in the post–World War II generation. I always kind of wanted to be in the military. I always liked and admired it. And it's something that I missed in a way—that I missed. But to say that I wished I'd gone would require me to rewrite history to an extraordinary extent."

———

August 1995:

"Whatever we may think about the political decisions of the Vietnam era, the brave Americans who fought and died there had noble motives. They fought for the freedom, and the independence of the Vietnamese people."

———

July 1995:

"I believe normalization and increased contact between Americans and Vietnamese will advance the cause of freedom in Vietnam just as it did in eastern Europe and the former Soviet Union. I strongly believe that engaging the Vietnamese on the broad economic front of economic reform, and the broad front of democratic reform, will help to honor the sacrifice of those who fought for freedom's sake in Vietnam.''

———

July 11, 1995

''By helping to bring Vietnam into the community of nations, normalization also serves our interest in working for a free and peaceful Vietnam in a stable and peaceful Asia.''

———

The Personal Side

"When you're young, you think you're going to live forever."

———

1993:

"Some days I feel like the oldest forty-six-year-old man in history."

———

After admiring a reporter's large-numeral watch, he was asked if he needed one himself:

"I don't know. My eyes are getting worse. For most of my life I had better than 20/20 vision. But all of a sudden, in the last three or four years, my lenses started flattening, and I can't read, and it's just awful—it really is. My primary manifestation of age, except for getting gray, gray, gray."

———

1996:
Memphis, Tennessee, August 31, 1996:

"And you know, I just turned fifty, and Al [Gore] never lets me forget about it. And I got my AARP card, you know. I'm a certified old guy now."

———

When asked how old he felt on his fiftieth birthday:

". . . in my body and my spirit, I felt about thirty-five. In my head, I sometimes feel eighty-five."

———

"Becoming fifty gives me more yesterdays than tomorrows, and I'll now begin to think more about the long-term implications as well as the consequences of what I do."

On the impact of turning fifty:

"I think a lot of people have mixed feelings when they get to be fifty. From my point of view, I am very glad to be alive. My father died in his late twenties, so I feel that I have already received more gifts in life and from life than most people ever do. I felt an enormous sense of gratitude, and I began to think about the next phase of my life and what it would be like—the whole aging process—in a very positive light. I think, in a way, it is a blessing. You have to take it as a gift, not a curse."

ARKANSAS

February 1993:

"Growing up in Arkansas gave me a sense of security and responsibility that comes from community and the feeling of belonging. It emphasized the importance of balance in human independence, self-reliance, and generosity of spirit.

"In Arkansas I learned pride in the well-made thing and reverence for all God's creation. I learned to love my country and feel a duty to my neighbor. I learned to love learning and believe it was the foundation of personal and collective progress.

"You can find the kinds of people who taught me what I most value in every part of America, but I first discovered them and learned from them as a child in Arkansas, and it is a part of the reason I cherish it so."

"If you travel its roads and visit its towns, as I have done countless times, you'll discover Arkansas is a glorious mosaic. There's enormous variety in its terrain— farmland, wetlands, woodlands, foothills, mountains. There are folks of every background and interest. Their humor and hospitality will warm your heart."

———

On leaving Arkansas for Washington after being elected president:
"Yeah. I love this place. You know, I love the state, I love the city. This has been our home for twelve of the last fourteen years. I loved my job. It is not easy for me to leave. I have deep roots here. But I don't think it's so bad for the American people to have a president who hates to leave his home. I think that's probably good."

———

"There was a story going around Arkansas last fall that I would try to stay on as governor even if I were elected president. It was a gentle joke."

"You can't know me and fail to notice how much I love Arkansas: the people, the landscape, the towns, their histories."

———

BOOKS

"When it comes to children, the first teachers must always be their parents . . . I urge all of America's parents, make sure there are books beneath your Christmas tree. Share the joy of reading as a family."

———

"Let me say to our parents: You have to lead the way. Every tired night you spend reading a book to your child will be worth it many times over. I know that Hillary and I still talk about the books we read to Chelsea when we were so tired we could hardly stay awake. We still remember them. And, more important, so does she."

———

"The public library, by giving every citizen equal access to books and learning, allows us to preserve this great system of participatory democracy. Libraries are the centers for free and equal access to the information needed to govern. Public libraries are also essential in our educational system. They provide safe haven for personal growth and offer a much-needed sense of community. They are the peoples' university for self-education, and they support literacy and learning activities in every stage of life. Everything that makes this country great—our history, our government, our people, and our freedom—is available through the variety of books, information, and services that libraries provide."

———

Food

"I don't necessarily consider McDonald's junk food. You know, they have chicken sandwiches, they have salads."

———

At a breakfast at the White House:

"I love hosting these breakfasts. It's the only time they let me eat eggs."

———

"Those of us who came of age when Eisenhower was our father figure and then the torch was passed to Kennedy, who grew up believing in the legacy of World War II, with Franklin Roosevelt and Harry Truman, politics was an honorable, not a dishonorable profession."

———

"I think for a lot of people in my generation, a lot of our adulthood has been about trying to keep what was great about the sixties alive and to grow out of what was wrong."

———

"Life has always been difficult and challenging, and this is just our generation's moment. And we need to do it. We need to quit bellyaching and do it."

———

"I have friends in Washington who I supposed would be classified as hippies or members of the off-beat generation. There has been, I think, in the hippie movement in this country a good deal of rather unhealthy negativism. There are many hippies I know who are highly ethical. They see a lot of contradictions in our society, and they can't find the answers. I have no quarrel with them. If they find self-expression in being hippies, then I think they have every right to act the way they feel. I don't think they are unhealthy for our society."

———

1993:

"I often feel like Wile E. Coyote, trying to achieve the impossible."

————

On what went through his mind when an old speech to Congress flashed up on the TelePrompTer as he began his health-care address:

"I thought to myself, 'That was a pretty good speech, but not good enough to give twice.'"

————

Addressing the Presidential Scholars, a group of high-school honor students, at Constitution Hall in Washington, July 1, 1996:

"This has been sort of a crazy week around here.

"I was hoping maybe one of the scholars could explain chaos theory."

————

In Denver, after hecklers interrupted his speech, October 30, 1996:

"Look, you shouldn't be too upset about that. You know what Mark Twain said about that? He said every dog needs a few fleas. Now, I'll admit, I've had a few more than I wanted. But Mark Twain said every dog needs a few fleas. It keeps him from worrying so much about being a dog."

————

"It reminds me of my other favorite dog story. You know, this guy is going down the highway and he sees this sign that says

'George Jones, Veterinarian-Taxidermist.' Either way you get your dog back.''

Presidential Luncheon, Cobo Conference and Exhibition Center, Detroit, Michigan, March 4, 1996:

"I also want to thank David Bonior for telling that joke. I used to tell jokes, but they told me it wasn't presidential, so I had to quit. So now I just have to laugh at other people, and I'm always grateful when I get one."

Women's Leadership Forum, July 17, 1996:

"Sometimes I hate to be last, you know. The very first speech I ever gave as a public official, twenty years ago, January of 1977, I was attorney general. I went to a Rotary Club installation banquet. It's one of these deals that starts at 6:30 P.M.; there were five hundred people there. Everybody in the crowd but four people got introduced; they went home mad. I got up to talk at a quarter to 10:00 P.M. And the guy that introduced me was the only person there more nervous than me, and the first words out of his mouth was, 'You know, we could stop here and have had a very nice evening.'

"Now, he didn't mean it that way. At least I don't think he did. But we could stop here and have had a very nice evening."

Visiting a General Motors truck assembly plant in Shreveport, Louisiana:

"I've been trying to think of a diplomatic way to ask for one of these pickup trucks behind me.

196

"When I was a younger man and had a life, I owned an El Camino pickup in the seventies . . . It had Astroturf in the back. You don't want to know why, but I did."

———

You Can Take the Boy Out of Arkansas . . . But

During 1992 campaign:

"I'll be there for you 'til the last dog dies."

———

Declaring that the government:

". . . ought to give people a good lettin' alone on things that are truly private."

———

"Even a blind hog can find an acorn."

———

"The only thing I can tell you is that everything I ever suspicioned about the way the federal government operates turned out to be true, plus some."

———

PHILOSOPHY

"I tell people around here all the time that if you just get up and dress and show up for the game, you're going to win some. I mean, I just keep trying to remind everybody here, even in the toughest times, that if what you want to do is right, and if you will work with diligence and keep your ears open to that you can learn from the mistakes, in the end your efforts are more likely to be successful than not, because, in the end, the reason these things work is because they're needed. History calls for certain movements—and, particularly in the life of a democracy like this, from the grass roots up—because they are needed. So I really believe there's something to be said for having this sort of dogged perseverance, which has been remarked on in the past, because nobody ever promised me or anyone else it should be easy."

———

"I do have core principles, and I do my best to live by them. I don't think you can be a great president unless you have both conviction and the capacity to change things. But I measure my worth in the job I have done, not just by espousing core principles and making all the right enemies, but in effecting change."

———

"If you live in that kind of constant environment where conflict is never resolved, you tend to repeat that pattern when you grow up. That was an early problem with me, so that I would let things fester too long and then try to deal with them in an emergency situation. Now I think I do a much better job of just dealing with life as it comes along."

———

"All my life, I've had to work to draw the line in the dirt, to make conflict my friend, not my enemy."

———

"I'm a lot like Baby Huey. I'm fat. I'm ugly. But if you push me down, I keep coming back. I just keep coming back."

"The trick is to be firm on your principles and direction and flexible in dealing with people who have the power either to help you further that direction or to derail it. I mean, it's interesting. Compromise is very often given a bad name in popular circles today. And yet our system was set up to mandate compromise in ways that most governmental democracies weren't."

———

Sioux Falls, South Dakota, November 4, 1996:

"When we join hands and run our country the way you try to run your families, your churches, your farms, your factories, your businesses, your communities, your charities, when we do that we always win. There is no person living in this country today who knows that better than I do. There is no person living in this country today who has been given more gifts, who feels more humble on this night than I do."

———

Second presidential debate, San Diego, California, October 16, 1996:

"I have a simple philosophy that I've tried to follow for the last four years—do what creates opportunity for all, what reinforces responsibility from all of us, and what will help us build a community where everybody has got a role to play and a place at the table."

———

"I have concluded a few things in my life and one of them is that you don't ever get even. The harder you try, the more frustrated

199

you're going to be, because nobody ever gets even. And when you do, you don't feel fulfilled."

———

January 1997:

Asked if there were a wish he would share with the American people for 1997:

"My wish would be that we could all come closer to living like Cardinal Bernardin's admonition in the last speech he gave right before he died, when he said that life is too short to waste the precious gift of time on acrimony and division. He said that knowing he did not have many days left on this Earth. An astonishing man, Cardinal Bernardin. But that would be my wish—that we could live by that wish."

———

RELIGION

"I have never stopped believing in God. I never stopped feeling better in those big churches in England. But it wasn't anything that guided my life. Religious faith for me now is sort of humbling and provides an incredible amount of protection. But for my faith, I don't know that I'd ever been able to forgive myself for the things I've done wrong in my life. I'm also not sure that I would care about the work I do."

———

"We need our faith . . . as a source of humility, to remember that, as Bishop Sheen said, we are all sinners."

———

Address at U.S. Botanical Gardens, Washington, D.C., April 21, 1993:

"All across this country, there is a deep understanding rooted in our religious heritage and renewed in the spirit of this time that the bounty of nature is not ours to waste. It is a gift from God that we hold in trust for future generations. Preserving our heritage, enhancing it, and passing it along is a great purpose worthy of a great people. If we seize the opportunity and shoulder the responsibility, we can enrich the future and ennoble our own lives."

———

"I really believe in a lot of the old-fashioned things like the constancy of sin, the possibility of forgiveness, and reality of redemption. And I believe it in a Baptist way—that a lot of a person's spiritual journey should be intensely private and shared only with God."

———

"I came to see my church as a place not for saints but for sinners, for people who know they're weak, not who pretend to be strong."

———

"If I didn't believe in God, if I weren't, in my view, a Christian, if I didn't believe ultimately in the perfection of life after death, my life would have been much more difficult for me. I had a tough childhood, a not all that easy adulthood at times. My faith has enabled me to keep living and keep going and keep doing things."

———

"The fact that I have a deep faith in God and a sense of trying to do the right thing every day should be reassuring to people. It will make me more humble in office. It will make me a stronger person.''

———

At White House prayer breakfast, October 6, 1993:

''The fact that we have freedom of religion doesn't mean we need to try to have freedom from religion. It doesn't mean that those of us who have faith shouldn't frankly admit that we are animated by that faith, that we try to live by it, and it does affect what we feel, what we think, and what we do.''

———

''The Bible is the authoritative Word of God and contains all truth. There are people who read the same Bible, have the same convictions about its authority, and draw different conclusions.''

———

''My faith tells me all of us are sinners, each of us is gone in our own way and fallen short of the glory of God, and that life's struggle is for sinners, not saints, for the weak, not the strong. Religious faith has permitted me to believe in the continuing possibility of becoming a better person every day, to believe in the search for complete integrity in life.''

———

Asked if he believes in life after death:

''Yeah, I have to. I need a second chance.''

———

"I really do believe in the constancy of sin, the constant possibility of forgiveness, the reality of redemption and the promise of a future life. But I'm also a Baptist who believes that salvation is primarily personal and private, that my relationship is directly with God and not through any intermediary. Other people can have different views, and I've spent a good part of my life trying to understand the different religious views, celebrate them and figure out what brings us together."

———

"Don't forget this country was founded on a belief in religious liberty. A lot of the first people who came to the shores of the United States came here because they wanted to come to a place where nobody would tell them how to worship God, and they could make their own mind up."

———

State of the Union Address, January 23, 1996:

"I applaud the work of religious groups that care for the poor. More than anyone else, they know the difficulty of this task, and they are in a position to help. Every one of us should join with them."

———

"If you have a religious faith that changes your life and makes you a better person, it also makes you more respectful of other people."

———

"The reason this country still has such a vibrant and profoundly religious bent is that we have protected the right of all faiths and we've welcomed others to our shores who are not only not Christians or Jews or Muslims but also Buddhists, Shintoists, other people who have different faiths."

SLEEP

"Every major error I made in my life I made when I was really tired."

————

May 1996:

"I realized after about six months here that I was too often on edge. And it was because I was trying to carry a different order of magnitude of decision than I had previously. Now, if I don't get six hours, it's not enough. And a lot of times, I'll stay in bed seven hours, which is—it's an eternity for me in my lifetime."

————

SPORTS

"Growing up in Arkansas, we had good basketball teams in high school, but football was always the Southern sport."

————

"In Arkansas, when I was a kid, everybody loved football. Basketball didn't really catch on until I was a young man, not until Eddie Sutton came up and decided to coach basketball. He and his wife became friends of Hillary's and mine, and I learned most of what I know about basketball from him. He went on to Kentucky and then to Oklahoma State, and he's the only coach to take four different teams to the N.C.A.A. So I became a great basketball nut. I still love football, and I love golf, and I love the Olympics."

"I tried to learn how to play tennis. But I just wasn't very good at it. Hillary's always been a better tennis player; she's quit playing, which I think is a great mistake, because she has a gift for it. I've been trying to get her to start playing again."

———

Meeting with then prime minister of Canada, Brian Mulroney in 1993:

"It is worth noting that the United States and Canada share the world's longest undefended border and that we haven't had a battle between us since the War of 1812. Now, having said that, Mr. Prime Minister, I will tell you that I look forward to winning back the World Series."

———

Speech to 1995 World Series Champion Atlanta Braves, February 26, 1996:

"This is a happy day for all of us. Three years ago, shortly after I became president, I had occasion to meet the Canadian prime minister when he hosted a meeting in Vancouver between President Yeltsin and me. And he wanted to have all this high-flowing policy discussion, and I said, 'Now, before anything else, I want to tell you that my number one objective in our relations with Canada is to win the World Series back.' And I want to thank the Atlanta Braves for helping my foreign policy with Canada to succeed."

———

Speech at Orioles Stadium, Baltimore, Maryland, April 2, 1996:

"I went down to see the umpires before the game, and I said that I really wanted to see them because they were the only people in the country that got second-guessed more than I did. So I like those guys. I'm for them, you know. They are the company misery loves."

On basketball:

"It's a fabulous game, isn't it? It makes me wish I were two inches taller and twenty pounds lighter. With a four-foot vertical jump, I could be doing something else."

On the Arkansas Razorbacks:

"If you want to be calm and quiet, you should not watch a game with me. I call the Hog. I change the defenses. I talk to all the players. I do all kinds of stuff. But it's a great tension-reliever."

"I think that America likes March Madness and likes college basketball as much as anything else because it is both an individual and a team sport. And it has both rules and creativity; discipline and energy. And in that sense, it is sort of a symbol of what's best about our country when things are going well.

"And I hope we can all remember that. We all need to live with rules and creativity, with discipline and energy, and we all need to remember that, however good any of us are, we're all on a team. And when we're on the team, the team's doing well, the rest of us, we do pretty well individually."

Speech at banquet honoring Dr. and Mrs. Billy Graham, May 2, 1996:

"The first time I ever met Paul Harvey, he and his son played through a foursome I was in on this golf course in Chicago. He never told me the score. But since then he's tried to tell the score about a lot of other things. And I've enjoyed it every time."

———

After golfer Greg Norman told reporters that the president was beating him in a golf game in Australia:

"If you believe that, I've got some land I want to sell you."

———

From a 1988 interview about how he got started running:

"I have a family history of being overweight and having heart trouble, and running will help me beat the odds. And it's good for me psychologically because I can get out and think a little."

———

"As governor, I ran five days a week, three miles on weekdays and longer on the weekends."

———

"Running helps me stay on an even keel and in an optimistic frame of mind. No matter how bad I feel or how bad the news is, if I can go out and run, I always feel better."

———

"Traveling has made it much more difficult for me to run, and I'm running much less than I wish I could. I've also gained 'bout twenty pounds, but if I can get back to fifteen or twenty miles a week, I can get my weight down to normal."

———

On jogging in the humidity of a Washington summer in 1993:

"Now I can lose another ten pounds."

———

TRAVEL IN THE UNITED STATES

White House Conference on Travel and Tourism, October 30, 1995:

"This industry has been near and dear to my heart since I was a little boy. I grew up in a resort town that also embraced a national park. As an adult I've had the good fortune to travel a fair amount, although as president I must say one of the more frustrating aspects of the job is I go to a lot of interesting places and never get to be a tourist."

———

Campaign train 1996:

"I'm taking a train through the heartland because I want to look into eyes and faces and hearts of people like you."

———

"Yesterday, Chelsea and I started out with Hillary in West Virginia. We went into Kentucky, then we came into Ohio. We've had a wonderful day on this train. I wanted to take this train

208

through the heartland to Chicago because I wanted to see people like you, the people I've been working for for the last four years, on the way to accept for the second time the nomination of my party for president.

"I also—I also very much wanted you to see us on this train because it's not only on the right track to Chicago, this train is on the right track to the twenty-first century, and I want you to keep us on it."

———

Grand Canyon National Park, September 18, 1996:

"Ladies and gentlemen, the first time I ever came to the Grand Canyon was also in 1971 in the summer. And one of the happiest memories of my entire life was when, for some fluky reason, even in the summertime, I found a place on a rock overlooking the Grand Canyon where I was all alone. And for two hours I sat and I lay down on that rock and I watched the sunset. And I watched the colors change layer after layer after layer for two hours. I could have sat there for two days if the sun had just taken a little longer to set.

"And even today, twenty-five years later, in hectic, crazy times, in lonely, painful times, my mind drifts back to those two hours that I was alone on that rock watching the sunset over this canyon. And it will be with me till the day I die. I want more of those sights to be with all Americans for all time to come."

———

Chicago, on Hillary's recent travels in Central and Eastern Europe, July 2, 1996:

"She was bragging on her day in Romania. She said, well, I've been in Romania. I'm going to the Czech Republic. I'm going to

209

Hungary. I'm going to Poland. I'm going to Estonia. And she said she was going to a couple of other places. And I said, well, I'm going to Chicago, and I'll see people from all those places with just one stop. And I said you could have stayed home and done all that with a lot less effort, you know.''

———

Campaign 1996

"Now it is time to look to the challenges of today and tomorrow. Our nation was built on challenges, not promises. When we work together to meet them, we never fail. That is the key to a more perfect union: our individual dreams must be realized by our common efforts."

January 6, 1996

"The American people have decided that it is better for people to work than be on welfare; that welfare should be a temporary help, not a way of life, but that the solution should support children and families, not undermine them. Americans have decided they want a smaller government that is less bureaucratic and more creative, that serves them as well or better with less money, and that there should be a tax cut that promotes educational opportunity and strengthens the ability of families to care for their children.

"Now we can achieve these goals. We can balance the budget while remaining true to these values. This is a great challenge, but not the greatest one we have faced. It is not the financial numbers that are blocking our progress. It is political ideology. It is time now to do what our parents have done before us—to put the national interests above narrow interests.

"I'm not much of a lame-duck type. It's not in my makeup. So I expect that I will be hitting it full-time until the last day I'm here."

"My fellow Americans—this must be a campaign of ideas, not a campaign of insults. The American people deserve it.

"Four years from now, just four years from now—think of it—we begin a new century, full of enormous possibilities. We have

212

to give the American people the tools they need to make the most of their God-given potential. We must make the basic bargain of opportunity and responsibility available to all Americans, not just a few. That is the promise of the Democratic Party. This is the promise of America.

"I would like to be the second president in the history of the country, the first was Theodore Roosevelt, with some help from Woodrow Wilson at the end, to lead this country through a period of dramatic change within America and in the world without a major war. It's only happened once before in our country's history, and I'd like that to be my legacy."

August 1996

"So I said to Al Gore tonight, I said, 'Man, I'm dog-tired. Why in the world are we getting on that bus tomorrow? Why aren't we taking our kids to the Shedd Aquarium tomorrow? Why aren't we sort of just chilling out tomorrow?'

"And he looked at me with that inevitable sense of humor of his and he dead-panned, 'We do not want Mr. Dole to be president of the United States.' So I said, 'Okay, but when I get up in the morning and I'm whining about this and talking about how I'm older than you are and I hurt everywhere, just say that again so I'll remember why I'm doing this.' "

"I would agree that I've grown in office. I think it happened through the crucible of decision making and through the fights that we had to fight, through the victories as well as the defeats and also, I think, through the human losses, which are very humbling, both our personal losses, Hillary's and mine, and the losses the country sustained."

"I have a lot of things I want to do. As a matter of fact, I've thought a lot about second-term presidencies, and some of them haven't worked out so well, and I believe that they haven't worked out so well because the presidents ran for reelection and got reelected just because people were satisfied with the job they'd done, but they didn't have an agenda, which is why I went to the trouble to write a book about what I wanted to do in my next term, to lay out a lot of very specific things at my speech at the Democratic convention. When I go around the country, I talk about how we're going to balance the budget, how we're going to make college available to all, how we're going to build on the anticrime efforts, and how we're going to implement welfare reform. I have a whole lot of things I really want to do in the next four years to complete this transformation of our nation into the twenty-first century."

———

Presentation of Henry Ossawa Tanner painting, October 29, 1996:

"Tonight is a happy night for us, to be here, to be a part of this. Tonight reminds us, in all humility, that we are simply tenants here passing through—even though we're trying to get our lease renewed at the moment. There is, in any case, a limit on the lease, and it's a very short period in the very long life of our great country."

———

"This is my last election unless I run for the school board someday."

214

Bob Dole

Asked about differences between himself and Dole:

"I think there are perhaps two or three. One is you could see in our convention speeches I want to build a bridge to the future, and he said he wanted to build a bridge back to the past. I believe we're better off when we work together to create the conditions that give people the tools to make the most of their own lives. I think he believes normally you're better off when you're on your own. He said specifically at the convention—he took my wife and her book on when he said it doesn't take a village. Well, I think it does take a village. I think his life is evidence that it takes a village. I think that the whole story of his life is the support system that goes beyond individual and family endeavor and has other people coming in to help make the most of your own life. And I think that's Bob Dole's story, and I know it's mine."

At a Washington fund-raiser:

"Say you were going on vacation for a couple of weeks. Who do you trust to water your plants—Bob Dole or Bill Clinton?"

Women's Leadership Forum, July 17, 1996:

"I was asked the other night on an interview program that I did for the new television network to name a quality—a caller called in on e-mail and said, tell me what you admire most about Senator Dole. And I said, well, I don't just admire one thing about Senator Dole, I admire a lot of things. But the thing I think I like the most about him is I really believe he loves America. And I believe that. I don't think we need to run a hateful campaign and demean the

215

people who are our opponents, and try to do that. I don't believe in that."

———

Asked about Dole's age, if it should be an issue:

"No, I think the age of his ideas should be an issue. I think that people should evaluate which one of us can best lead into the future.

"I want to run on the differences in our ideas and our records, not on his age."

———

"I want to thank Senator Dole for something. He made a great speech for my reelection the other day. You know, we had a report we were at 10.5 million new jobs in the last four years. And then last week it came out that we had another 210,000 new jobs, for 10.7 million jobs—faster job growth than any Republican administration since the 1920s. And when that happened, Senator Dole said we had the worst economy in twenty years.

"Now, why is that a speech? Because just two weeks before he said we had the worst economy in a hundred years. Now, who else do you know who could make up eighty years in two weeks? We're moving in the right direction."

———

ACCOMPLISHMENTS

"Even when I was doing the right things, I'm not sure I communicated it as clearly as I should have. I think I'm doing a better job of that now."

———

In 1995, the White House released a sixteen-page list of accomplishments:

"If you'd told me two years ago that I could have accomplished all these things and still be in trouble, I wouldn't have believed you."

"We have continued to expand opportunities in education and to continue to invest. We have increased our investment in infrastructure by about ten percent while reducing the deficit, something that I know is important to all of you. And the American people have produced 9.7 million new jobs in three and a half years."

CAMPAIGN ISSUES 1996

Business

1992:

"Nonetheless, it is still true that it matters who owns significant chunks of your economy. You need a manufacturing base in your own country. That requires domestic policies which reward the companies that are here in research and development and don't subsidize the flight of those jobs overseas."

1993:

"What we are seeing is that over the long run, the companies that win are going to be the ones who treat their workers like partners, who involve them in the company to give them a sense of ownership in the enterprise, and who understand that that's the most important asset we've got."

217

———

On corporate responsibility:

"I want to bring these people together and let them talk about how doing the right things—stabilizing income, stabilizing jobs, providing certain benefits—has enabled them to make more money, not less, and how you can do right and do well at the same time."

———

Small Business:

"The vitality of the small-business sector is one reason we have a lower unemployment rate than all of our competitors except Japan."

———

"Everybody knows the problems of campaign money today: there's too much of it, it takes too much time to raise, and it raises too many questions."

———

"It's going to be difficult for us to pass the kind of health-care reforms we need and the kinds of budgetary changes we need, unless we can pass campaign-finance and lobby reform."

———

At a January 1997 news conference regarding the controversy over contributions in the 1996 campaign:

". . . way over ninety percent . . . of the money that was raised . . . was raised in a perfectly lawful fashion."

———

Interview by Tabitha Soren of MTV, Aboard the MTV Choose or Lose Bus, August 30, 1996:

"But I say this—there's never been any attempt to raise any money with the promise that you can spend the night in the Lincoln Bedroom. I have invited people who have been helpful to me to spend the night in the Lincoln Bedroom, but it was never a quid pro quo there."

———

On overnight guests at the White House:

"I just simply disagree that it is wrong for a president to ask his friends and supporters to spend time with him."

———

On White House coffees for political donors:

"I enjoyed them enormously . . . I still believe as long as there was no specific price tag put on those coffees—just the fact that [guests] would later be asked to help the president or the party does not render them improper."

———

Entitlements

1992:

"What I explicitly said was that I thought the way to reform the entitlements was to make upper-income recipients pay more of their load, but that I thought the universality of the entitlement programs was important. It may be an important symbolic issue of fairness to ask older people with higher incomes to pay more for Medicare and to subject most or all of their income from Social Security to taxation. I think you can make that case pretty plainly, that it's important symbolically. But more than that is getting control of health-care costs."

1993: *On talk entitlement budget will be cut more:*

"It not only could, but it should . . . We must deal with entitlements, especially Medicare and Medicaid. If we don't, in a few years, being in Congress will be a matter of just writing checks for more of the same health care and of paying interest on the debt. We have cut defense all we can, and we've put a freeze on aggregate domestic spending. Entitlements, especially health care—that's the next step."

———

1994:

"Behind every one of these entitlements there is a person. It is the middle-class entitlements that have united us and brought us together."

———

Families

Speechwriter Paul Begala and his wife were expecting during the 1992 campaign. The Clintons told him to go home and stay there:

"Don't leave her side, no matter what. The most important thing in your life is to be there.

"It's a gift my father never lived to see."

———

The Family Leave Bill:

"The first bill I am to sign as president truly puts people first. I am very appreciative that the Congress has moved so rapidly."

———

"I think that work is very important, and obviously the work in which we are engaged is supremely important to us. But all of it only counts insofar as it enables you to live a better life. A lot of people in this country today can't even have this debate.

"I think about how hard it is for us just to take time out for each other or take time out for our daughter. And then I think about all these people out there where it's not even an option. Just to stay alive, they have to give up everything that's personal to them. For people who have the options, I would tell them: You shouldn't sacrifice the things that make your life unique, that nourish your personality, your basic relationships."

———

December 13, 1993:

"I think that parenting is the most important job in this society and the one that has been neglected most. I think having people with families work here makes for a place more in touch with the real world. So I'm concerned about it."

———

"What I want to do is get the country to a point where we realize we have to do some serious things about crime and violence, about putting families back together. But if you want to rebuild these communities, you can't do it in the absence of work. We have to build a kind of national consensus around reconstituting families and welfare reform and doing something about crime and violence that also says you have to be able to work."

———

"I think people know instinctively that if we can't succeed as parents and workers, then society is going to suffer either economically or socially."

———

"If you look at this great country of ours, and you ask, how can we come together instead of be driven apart, you have to start with our basic values. We need to build up families and the integrity and strength of child-rearing, not tear it down. That's why I've said many times, I'm all for welfare reform that's tough on work if people can work, but I don't want to hurt the children. We should be supportive of good parenting and work. All of us try to succeed as workers and parents. That's what we should want poor people to do, too. Everybody should be able to succeed in that way. That should be our goal."

———

Roundtable Discussion on Balancing Work and Family, Nashville, Tennessee, July 24, 1996:

"When Hillary and I and Al and Tipper all sort of moved into the White House, one of the things that I tried to do was to kind of get a fix on the people who were working for us. Now, a lot of people who work for the White House are young people who haven't started their families yet, and that's probably good because they work these crazy hours and they never seem to get tired. I used to be that way myself. And then a lot of people who work for us, all their children are grown, so they can accommodate bizarre schedules and long hours.

"But we have a significant number of people in very responsible positions who still have children who are either school age or preschool age. And one of the things I told them when we started this was that we were on a mission to change America for the better, but it wasn't as important as taking care of their kids. And if they ever thought that their families were really suffering, they ought to quit, because the most important job any of us have, starting with the president, is to be a good parent. And several of them have taken me up on my admonition—sometimes at great personal loss to me."

———

Second debate, San Diego, California, October 16, 1996:

"The most important good things that happen in America happen in families."

———

From acceptance speech, July 16, 1992:

"I want an America where 'family values' live in our actions, not just in our speeches."

———

"Sometimes, all of the answers have to come from the values that speak to us from within."

———

Tenth annual convention of the National Association of Hispanic Publications, National Press Club, January 26, 1996:

"I wanted to tell you that—I know Secretary Cisneros spoke yesterday, and he was to be here tonight, but his son is having a Cub Scout meeting—and Henry is the den leader. So we are trying to practice family values in our administration, and he's doing what he should be doing."

Jobs

1992:

"We are losing entirely too many manufacturing jobs because we have no strategy to deal with the productivity problems and the competition problems."

——

"I believe it's time for dramatic change in the workplace. We need policies that empower the American worker by providing the skills necessary for high-wage jobs; by guaranteeing every American a quality, affordable core package of health benefits; by ending deductions for outrageous CEO pay; and by rewarding pro-work and pro-family policies. Together, we can make America more productive and prosperous."

——

"It's time for a revolution in the workplace built around greater cooperation between labor and management and emphasizing more decision-making authority in the hands of front-line workers. My administration will end deductions for outrageous executive pay, encourage companies to provide for employee ownership and profit-sharing mechanisms, and permit shareholders to determine the compensation of top executives."

——

1996:

"We have gotten rid of the system people say they don't like. But if you want to require somebody with kids to feed to go to work, and require them to do it, they better have some work there to go to.

That is the issue now. We have a responsibility to create these jobs. And we have to build a bridge to the twenty-first century that puts people to work who have never had a chance to go to work before."

―――

Immigration

"When I ran for president, I think in some ways the most rewarding part of the experience was having the opportunity to see just how many different countries and how many different ethnic groups have contributed to making America what it is today. We don't want to do anything to interrupt that. But we cannot continue to progress as a country unless we have a more vigorous response to this problem. I mean, we cannot—and we don't want to cloud the two. This has nothing to do with our support for keeping the rainbow and the melting pot of America going and growing and enriching and strengthening this country.

"But the kinds of practices that are manifest in who can get into this country on an airplane, what kind of illegal smuggling can go on, and the fact that our borders leak like a sieve—those things cannot be permitted to continue in good conscience. It's not good for the American immigrants who are here legally in this country, for the American economy, for the cohesion of our society, or for the rule of law worldwide. And we're going to try to do better."

―――

"The simple fact is that we must not—and we will not—surrender our borders to those who wish to exploit our history of compassion and justice. We cannot tolerate those who traffic in human cargo, nor can we allow our people to be endangered by those who would enter our country to terrorize Americans. But the solution to the problem of illegal immigration is not simply to close our borders. The solution is to welcome legal immigrants and legal legitimate refugees, and to turn away those who do not obey the laws. We must say no to illegal immigration so we can continue to say yes to legal immigration."

———

"Our nation was built by immigrants. People from every region of the world have made lasting and important contributions to our society. We support legal immigration. In fact, we're doing what we can to speed up the process for people who do apply for citizenship when they're here legally. But we won't tolerate immigration by people whose first act is to break the law as they enter our country. We must continue to do everything we can to strengthen our borders, enforce our laws, and remove illegal aliens from our country.

"As I said in my State of the Union Address, we are a nation of immigrants, but we're also a nation of laws. And it is wrong, and ultimately self-defeating, for a nation of immigrants to permit the kind of abuse of our immigration laws we have seen in recent years."

———

"A hundred years ago we knew we were a nation of immigrants. And a hundred years later, we dare not forget it."

———

Democratic National Convention Reception, Philadelphia, Pennsylvania, September 25, 1996:

"And I saw a little piece of America there. I shook hands with a woman who had just come to live in the United States and her child, and she said, 'This could only happen in your country.' She said, 'I've only been here three months. I've just moved here from Hong Kong.' I thought, what an amazing thing, you know. We sometimes forget what a remarkable place the United States is and how real the Statue of Liberty is in the lives of so many millions of our people, and how the president is essentially the nation's hired hand, and is and should be accessible to all kinds of people from all walks of life and all stations. So we had a nice little visit and she likes Philadelphia."

Prayer in Public Schools

"It appears that some school officials, teachers, and parents have assumed that religious expression of any type is either inappropriate, or forbidden altogether, in public schools."

"What we have to do is to work together to help all Americans understand exactly what the First Amendment does. It protects freedom of religion by allowing students to pray and it protects freedom of religion by preventing schools from telling them how and when and what to pray. The First Amendment keeps us all on common ground."

"Americans should never have to hide their faith, but some Americans have been denied the right to express their religion, and that has to stop. The First Amendment does not—I will say again, does not—convert our schools into religion-free zones.

"I . . . believe the First Amendment as it is presently written permits the American people to do what they need to do."

Teen Pregnancy

1992 campaign:

"As president, I'll see that [young people] get the same deal everyone should have: play by the rules, stay off drugs, stay in school, and stay off the streets. Don't have children if you're not prepared to support them, because governments don't raise children, people do."

Asked if he believes it's immoral to have children out of wedlock:

"If someone becomes pregnant and decides to have a baby rather than have an abortion, that may be a moral decision, so I wouldn't say that everybody who becomes pregnant out of wedlock who has a baby is immoral. But I believe that this country would be a lot better off if children were born to married couples. Remember the Dan Quayle speech? There were a lot of very good things in that speech. The Murphy Brown thing was a mistake. It was too cute because this woman is not symbolic of the real problem in society. Would we be a better-off society if babies were born to married couples? You bet we would."

Visit to Kramer Junior High School in southeast Washington, April 25, 1994:

"I'm trying to do everything I can to give you more hope and more possibility for the future. But I can't lead your life for you. Every day you have to decide whether to be on time or not, whether to attend classes, whether to take drugs, whether to do your homework. And I'll be honest with you. The very best thing you can do to stay out of poverty is to make up your mind to wait to have a baby till you're old enough to take care of it and until you're married. You young men who get a girl pregnant and just walk away from her—you know it's wrong. It'll haunt you and stay with you all your life.''

———

"That was a tough audience. Afterwards a girl came up to me, probably about fourteen, and showed me a picture of her baby. What I talked about is real life for these kids.''

———

Television

On the V-chip in 1995:

"This is not censorship. This is parental responsibility.''

———

At the White House Office of Women's Initiatives "At the Table" Meeting, October 1996:

"I don't care what anybody says, I think being plugged into hundreds and hundreds of hours of televised murders numbs people to violence . . . We passed a requirement that new televisions have to come equipped with a V-chip that the parent can program to block out channels that aren't appropriate for your children . . . we are working on trying to do the equivalent of the V-chip on computers . . . Everything that is good and exciting about the modern world for your children has a flip side that creates a whole new series of security problems.''

———

Asked what he watches on TV, March 1996:

"I don't get to watch much. I normally watch specific movies or sporting events or news. Last night I tried to watch about an hour of the Grammys, because Chelsea joked I've missed twenty years of music and I need to get my head right . . . Anyway, I was trying to become somewhat less irrelevant to my own daughter and the other teenagers of the world."

———

Meeting top TV executives to discuss children's programming and ratings system:

"I'm someone who has a deep emotional attachment to *Starsky and Hutch.*"

———

The TV rating system:

"I do not believe the government should have anything to do with developing the ratings system or implementing it. I think it has to be a private thing, just like the movie rating system."

———

To a 1996 meeting of TV executives:

"We're handing the TV remote control back to America's parents."

———

Terrorism

"The United States cannot and will not refuse to do what we believe is right. Terrorism is the enemy of our generation and we must prevail."

On Larry King Live, June 5, 1995:

"In light of what we've been through in Oklahoma City and with the World Trade Center, if we could succeed in bringing a comprehensive peace to the Middle East, and then we could bring the benefits of that peace to all people who live there, I believe that that would help us to defeat terrorism in all continents in the next century. I think it's a huge deal for all the people of the world."

"But we cannot let the terrible actions of a few terrible people frighten us any more than they already have. So reach out to one another and come together. We will triumph over those who would divide us. And we will overcome them by doing it together, putting our children first."

"My fellow Americans, during the long struggles of World War II and the Cold War, our nation stood fast for freedom. In our time, terrorism is the enemy of peace and freedom. America must not, and America will not, be driven from the fight against terrorism. In this effort every American must stand with the men and women of our Armed Services. Every American must stand against violence and hatred, and stand for dignity and tolerance, at home as well as abroad. We must honor the memory of those we have lost by upholding the ideals for which they lived and the mission for which they gave their lives."

Tobacco

"The students that I just met with from Woodbridge showed me an incredible collection of tobacco ads and trinkets, T-shirts, hats and other giveaways, and tobacco products, all of which were found right here in your community, and all of which your fellow students thought were enticing young people to smoke. Now you've got a group of students here and we recently—just before I came out, I talked with students in eleven cities throughout the country, all of whom are committed to turning this around. And I know that in many ways the influence of young people on their peers is far greater than the influence of older people, even the president— maybe especially the president."

Announcing new restrictions on sale and advertising of cigarettes:

"Joe Camel and the Marlboro Man will be out of our children's reach forever."

Trade

"The world has plainly benefited from the increasing value of world trade. It is difficult for a rich country to grow richer without being able to export and virtually impossible for a poor country to escape poverty."

McDonnell Douglas plant, Long Beach, California, February 23, 1996:

"So often when I hear people talk about trade, they act as if there are only two alternatives—we just open our borders and let what

232

happens happen, or we close our borders because we think we're not being treated fairly. There is another alternative, and it's the right one. We should be pushing for free, but fair trade; for tough, but fair trade."

―――

"Although [NAFTA] is unpopular with some people and organizations I admire and represent . . . I think we should go forward with it because it advances our interests, the interests of ordinary Americans, more than it undermines it."

―――

"[Our] workers are the most productive in the world. We can win if we have access to markets. That's what NAFTA gives us."

―――

Violence

"Violent crime and the fear it provokes are crippling our society, limiting personal freedom, and fraying the ties that bind us."

―――

State of the Union Address, January 25, 1994:

"As you demand tougher penalties for those who choose violence, let us also remember how we came to this sad point. In our toughest neighborhoods, on our meanest streets, in our poorest rural areas, we have seen a stunning and simultaneous breakdown of community, family, and work—the heart and soul of civilized society."

―――

"There are many rights [guaranteed by] our laws . . . but [victims] have certain rights that we are letting slip away. They include the right to go out to the playground and the right to walk to the corner without fear of gunfire, the right to go to school safely, and to sit by an open window."

———

Roundtable Discussion at the White House Leadership Conference On Youth, Drug Use and Violence, Eleanor Roosevelt High School, Greenbelt, Maryland, March 7, 1996:

"We talked about my election in Jacksonville, Florida. I never raised the issue of race because crime knows no race. Drugs know no color. And violence can touch anybody. But I'm convinced, in this country, the United States of America, who put a man on the moon, we can eradicate drugs from our neighborhood and eliminate violence from our communities."

———

Work

On why he pushes himself:

"You've got to show others you're working harder than they are."

———

"Work gives dignity to life. People need an education. They need a job. They need a future, to give dignity to life."

———

"There was way too much short-term profit-taking at the expense of workers in the 1980s."

State of the Union Address, January 23, 1996:

"As workers increase their hours and their productivity, employers should make sure they get the skills they need and share the benefits of the good years as well as the burdens of the bad ones. When companies and workers work as a team, they do better. And so does America."

Reelection

"I would like to say a special word of thanks to Senator Dole. And I ask you to join me in applause for his lifetime of service to the United States."

"And I thank Jack Kemp for his service to America and his devotion to the proposition that this is a country in which everyone should have a chance to live free and equal and to have a chance at success."

"Let me say, I had a good visit with Senator Dole not too long before he went out to speak. I thanked him for his love of our country, for his years of service. I applauded the campaign that he fought so bravely to the very last minute. I thanked him for the work we did together to advance the common cause of America. And on behalf of all Americans, I wish him well and Godspeed."

———

"The American people have spoken. They have affirmed our course."

———

"I never met a person in public life that didn't wish that he or she had gotten all the votes. So would I have liked a few more? Of course. But I'm very gratified by what happened."

"I think one of the things I've learned over the last four years is that you have to use all the tools of the presidency to galvanize and mobilize the country."

———

"I'm a more optimistic, more idealistic American than I was four years ago."

———

Ongoing Issues

Abortion

"Under the present Arkansas law, abortion is illegal when the unborn child can live outside its mother's womb. I support that. While I have also supported restrictions on public funding and a parental notification requirement for minors, I think the government should impose no further restrictions . . . I believe the decision on abortion should be the woman's, not the government's."

———

In July 1991 he addressed the National Women's Political Caucus in Washington about his views on abortion:

"I think the majority of the American people are with this group on the issue of choice. I am opposed to overturning *Roe v. Wade.* I think it's the right decision. I think we should leave it intact."

———

1992 campaign:

"Hear me now: I am not pro-abortion; I am pro-choice."

———

"My position has always been that abortion should be safe, legal, and rare."

———

Adoption

August 26, 1996:

"And last week, in the minimum-wage law we did something else that was good for families. I signed a bill that gives a $5,000 tax credit to any couple willing to adopt a child and give that child a good home and an even more generous one if the child is disabled. And it removed the barriers to cross-racial adoption. So now we can say there are hundreds of thousands of kids out there trapped in foster care, they need loving homes. We have now made it more economically feasible for people to really be pro-family for those kids, too. And I'm proud of that.''

———

AIDS

"These issues have just never been issues. To me, this was an issue I came to on almost completely human terms. I just think in the last few years, knowing people who had AIDS, having a friend die of AIDS, made a big difference. It just sort of made me more, I don't know, comfortable in dealing with it.''

———

DEFENSE

McDonnell Douglas plant, Long Beach, California, February 23, 1996:

"We have here an example of America doing what is necessary to preserve our security and to lead the world. It happens also to provide a large number of people good jobs and security for their families. Where the civilian aircraft are being made, we have a good example of America leading the world toward prosperity and providing economic security for families. And in both places it happened because there was a partnership.''

———

"Why do we have a strong defense today? To defend our immediate interests and our borders, but also because we learned in the twentieth century that if we want to keep America free and safe we have to stand up for freedom and safety and security and peace and prosperity around the world. We can't be the world's policeman. We can't be everywhere. We can't do everything. But when we can make a difference and when it is consistent with our values and our interests, we have to try. That's what the effort in Bosnia is all about.''

DEMOCRACY

''Our greatest strength is the power of our ideas, which are still new in many lands. Across the world, we see them embraced— and we rejoice. Our hopes, our hearts, our hands, are with those on every continent who are building democracy and freedom. Their cause is America's cause.''

Moscow State University, Russia, May 10, 1995:

''First, the work of building democracy never ends. The democratic system can never be perfected, because human beings are not perfect.''

Commemoration of ''Fifty Years after Nuremberg: Human Rights and the Rule of Law,'' Gampel Pavilion, University of Connecticut, Storrs, Connecticut, October 15, 1995:

''Democracy is the best guarantor of human rights—not a perfect one, to be sure; you can see that in the history of the United States. But it is still the system that demands respect for the individual, and it requires responsibility from the individual to thrive. Democracy cannot eliminate all violations of human rights or outlaw human frailty, nor does promoting democracy relieve us of the obligation to press others who do not operate democracies to respect human rights. But more than any other system of government we know, democracy protects those rights, defends the victims of their abuse, punishes the perpetrators and prevents a downward spiral of revenge.''

———

Twenty-fifth anniversary of the Kennedy Center Honors, April 27, 1996:

''Recently the First Lady and I returned from a trip to the Far East and to Russia, and, as in other visits, we saw how prized an export our culture is. It's not just coincidence that it is embraced and adapted by a world increasingly sharing our democratic ideals. Visit almost any part of the world and there can be no doubt, our art, our music, our dance and theater are among our greatest ambassadors.''

———

Human Rights Day, December 10, 1996:

''History shows that nations where rights are respected and governments are freely chosen are more likely to be partners in peace and prosperity. That is why we've worked hard over the last four years to help equality and freedom take root in South Africa, to stop the reign of terror in Haiti, to promote reform in Bosnia and Russia, to bring freedom back to Bosnia, and peace, and to enable millions of suffering people all around the world to reclaim their simple human dignity. That is why we must continue to support the world's newest democracies and to keep the pressure on its remaining repressive regimes.''

———

''For the first time in history, more than half the world's people now live under governments of their own choosing. Today we dedicate ourselves to the unfinished task of extending freedom's reach. Promoting democracy and human rights reflects our ideals and reinforces our interests. It's a fundamental pillar of our foreign policy."

———

"We live at a time when our most deeply held ideals are ascendant, but this hopeful trend toward freedom and democracy is neither inevitable, nor irreversible, nor has it extended to the real lives of hundreds of millions of people all across the globe. While we seek to engage all nations on terms of goodwill, we must continue to stand up for the proposition that all people, without regard to their gender, their nationality, their race, their ethnic group or their religion, should have a chance to live up to their potential."

———

Second Inaugural Address, January 20, 1997:

"The world is no longer divided into two hostile camps. Instead, now we are building bonds with nations that once were our adversaries. Growing connections of commerce and culture give us a chance to lift the fortunes and spirits of people the world over. And for the very first time in all history, more people on this planet live under democracy than dictatorship."

———

DISCRIMINATION

During 1990 gubernatorial campaign, on a flight from Texarkana to Little Rock:

"I know how people are divided. I've seen it, I grew up with it. If there's anything I feel strongly about . . . it's that we can't let ourselves be torn apart like this."

246

Ebony, November 1995:

"I learned early on that segregation and discrimination of any kind weighed down all of us. As a son of the South, I know how impoverished we can be socially and spiritually when we deny the basic rights of citizenship to some of our people and when we separate our people from each other.

"The lesson we learned was a hard one. When we allow people to pit us against one another or spend energy denying opportunity based on our differences, everyone is held back. But when we give all Americans a chance to develop and use their talents, to be full partners in our common enterprise, then everybody is pushed forward."

Democratic National Convention, Chicago, Illinois, August 29, 1996:

"In our own country, we have seen America pay a terrible price for any form of discrimination. And we have seen us grow stronger as we have steadily let more and more of our hatreds and our fears go, as we have given more and more of our people the chance to live their dreams.

"That is why the flame of our Statue of Liberty, like the Olympic flame carried all across America by thousands of citizen heroes, will always, always burn brighter than the fires that burn our churches, our synagogues, our mosques, always."

DIVERSITY

1992:

"Perhaps the greatest responsibility of the next president is to bring our country together and to make our nation's rich diversity a source of strength, not weakness. When Americans have been united, we have been unstoppable. In recent years we have been divided by race, region, income and gender, with leaders who too often fail to recognize that we're all in this together.

"The president has the responsibility for setting the example of racial understanding and tolerance through his appointments to his staff and cabinet, by speaking out against racism and by taking affirmative steps to encourage communities to establish means for communicating on a regular basis across racial, ethnic and income lines."

———

Dedication ceremony, US Holocaust Museum, Washington, D.C., April 22, 1993:

"We must find in our diversity our common humanity. We must reaffirm that common humanity, even in the darkest and deepest of our own disagreements."

———

"We have worked throughout this entire life of our country to make our motto, *E pluribus unum*—from many, one—more than a slogan; instead, a driving force of unity and of strength. We have now to face the fact that we cannot achieve the first two objectives—liberty and freedom—or progress and prosperity—unless we can achieve the third, common ground.

"We established in our country a Constitution and a rule of laws, limitations of powers, separation of powers, authority at the state and local level. All these things were designed to give us a way to resolve our differences in a lawful, reconciling manner so that we could preserve our liberty and always make progress. It's worked pretty well for us for well over two hundred years now."

———

"If you look at the world and the problems it faces, and you look at home and the problems we face, it is clear that the responsibility of the United States today is to lead the world away from division; to show the world that the center can hold; that a free and diverse people, through democratic means, can form a lasting union. This is the challenge of our time and our responsibility as Americans."

"This country now has, more or less, two hundred different racial and ethnic groups. It's an astonishing thing that we can find ways to come together around our core values and our respect for one another's differences."

July 2, 1996:

". . . we've got to prove that the rest of the world is wrong when they fall out over race, religion and ethnicity. We've got to prove that we can be better and bigger than that—not because we're intrinsically better human beings, but because we've got a system and a history and a set of values in our Constitution that tells us how we ought to behave, and that we know from experience really works in the world of today and will work in the world of tomorrow."

DRUGS

On drug treatment on demand:

"Without it, the criminals will revert when they're released, and the problem will just get worse. Emphasizing treatment may not satisfy people fed up with being preyed upon, but a president should speak straight even if what he advocates isn't popular. If he sticks to his guns, the results will prove the wisdom of his policy."

———

"Drugs are deadly. Drugs are wrong. Drugs can cost you your life."

———

September 27, 1996:

". . . we ought to do more drug testing of people who are out on parole. Sixty percent of the cocaine and heroin consumed in the United States today is consumed by people who are already in the criminal-justice system in some way. You should not be on parole if you go back to drugs. That will make us a safer country."

———

Antidrug address to Maryland schoolchildren, March 3, 1997:

"I nearly lost my only brother. I'm not just telling you as the president. This is not a political speech; this is a personal statement."

———

"Drugs nearly killed my brother when he was a young man, and I hate them.

"He fought back. He's here tonight with his wife. His little boy is here. And I'm really proud of him."

———

EDUCATION

Speech to the Democratic Leadership Council, 1989:

"We must do more, better and differently than we have in the past. We have to have a nationful of Einsteins to stay even with the rest of the world."

———

October 1992:

"I believe we must promote lifetime learning for every American, investing in our people at every stage. We can start by fully funding Head Start and continue by investing in worker retraining programs for all workers and for individuals desiring to develop the necessary skills. We can specifically target America's urban youth by giving every American the opportunity to go to college through the establishment of a National Service Trust Fund. Those who borrow from the fund can pay it back either as a small percentage of their income over time, or through community service."

———

March 1993:

"A solid, comprehensive [education] program could do about as much to break the cycle and the mentality of dependency and poverty . . . as anything else we could do."

———

"We all know that Head Start, a program that prepares children for school, is a success story. We all know that it saves money, but today it just reaches barely over a third of all the eligible children. Under this plan, every eligible child will be able to get a head start. That is not just the right thing to do. It is the smart thing to do. For every dollar we invest today, we'll save three tomorrow.''

―――

". . . one of the most important parts of education is making sure that we tear down the artificial wall in every school system in America between what is academic and what is vocational.''

―――

ENVIRONMENT

1992:
Asked what he considers his greatest accomplishments in natural-resource conservation:

"One of my greatest accomplishments is preserving Arkansas's outstanding natural heritage. Arkansas offers some of the best fishing streams and lakes in the country; world-record brown trout were taken from the White and Little Red Rivers. Arkansas's forests are home to large populations of deer, turkey, and black bear.''

―――

Speech in Philadelphia, 1992:

"I've made the choice from time to time for jobs in a poor state. But I've learned something that George Bush and his advisers don't understand: to reject the false choice between economic growth and environmental protection. Today, you can't have a healthy economy without a healthy environment.''

―――

"You don't have to sacrifice environmental protection to get economic growth. The choice between jobs and environment is a false one: we can have both."

———

"If there is one commitment that defines our people, it is our devotion to the rich and expansive land we have inherited. From the first Americans to the present day, our people have lived in awe of the power, the majesty, and the beauty of the forests, the rivers, and the streams of America. That love of the land, which flows like a mighty current through this land and through our character, burst into service on the first Earth Day in 1970."

———

After vacationing in the Wyoming wilderness in 1995:

"We've seen breathtaking mountains, lakes, streams, and meadows. And all of this belongs to you, the American people, for all time to come."

———

"Because we believe that what God created we must not destroy, each of us has a sacred obligation to pass on a clean planet to future generations. For nearly three decades, all Americans have agreed we must do what we have to, to protect our environment. And America is cleaner and healthier because of it."

———

"Sometimes progress is measured in mastering frontiers, but sometimes we must measure progress in protecting frontiers for our children and all children to come."

Campaign speech at Monmouth Revolutionary War Memorial in Freehold, New Jersey, October 1996:

"I am not proud of the fact that there are still ten million American children living within four miles of a toxic-waste site. That is wrong. And if you give us four more years, we intend to clean up the five hundred worst sites so we can say America's children are growing up next to parks, not poison. Every child in America is entitled to that."

———

Great Falls National Park, April 22, 1996:

"You know, I just came back—literally just came back from a remarkable journey all around the world. I flew from here to Alaska and refueled, and then I went to Korea and Japan and on to St. Petersburg and Moscow. And I was thinking, standing here today, I saw some of the most magnificent man-made creations anywhere in the world: the Imperial Palace in Tokyo, the great Hermitage Museum in St. Petersburg, the entire Kremlin has just been redone and restored to its historical grandeur. But none of it is any more beautiful than this wonderful nature that God has given us right here in this national park."

———

"And not everybody can travel to see the great palaces of the world. Even the great art galleries of the world are beyond the reach of many of our fellow citizens. But everybody can come to this park without regard to their income, their station in life, what their other resources are. This belongs to all the American people, and we have to dedicate ourselves to making sure that as long as there is an America there will be a national park system with these treasures there for every single citizen of this country."

FREEDOM

To Foreign Policy Association, New York, New York, April 1, 1992:

"A second reality is that the irresistible power of ideas will shape the world in the Information Age. Television, cassette tapes and the fax machine helped ideas to pierce the Berlin Wall and bring it down. Look at the defining images of the past decade: Lech Walesa scaling the fence at the Lenin Shipyard; Vaclav Havel sounding the call for freedom at Wenceslas Square; Chinese students marching in Tienanmen Square, Nelson Mandela walking out of prison a free man; Boris Yeltsin standing defiantly atop a tank to face down the coup. These pictures speak of people willing to fight against all odds for their convictions, their freedom, and the right to control their own destiny."

———

"Have you ever noticed—it's very interesting, a lot of people want free speech for themselves, but don't believe in it for anyone else."

———

July 4, 1996:

"This is a day where all Americans put aside their business and their political preconceptions and just celebrate the freedom of our country; a day for family and friends, for softball and barbecue and music; a day to remember that even though we sometimes take the blessings of liberty for granted, millions of people around the world would give anything to share them."

———

Gun Control

Open letter from the president to hunters and sportsmen: April 29, 1994:

"I have been a hunter since I was twelve. Where I come from, it's a way of life. And I will not allow the rights of hunters and sportsmen to be infringed upon.

"But I know the difference between a firearm used for hunting and target shooting and a weapon designed to kill people. The nineteen specific types of assault weapons that would be banned by the proposal currently being considered in Congress have no place on a deer hunt, in a duck blind, or on a target range—and they certainly don't belong on our streets, in our neighborhoods, or on our schoolyards."

———

"I believe strongly in the right of Americans to own guns. I have used them as a hunter with great joy. But make no mistake, those who threaten the safety of others do not deserve our trust. If you're convicted of a felony, you shouldn't have one. If you're a fugitive from the law, you shouldn't have a gun. If you're stalking or harassing women or children, you shouldn't have a gun. And if you commit an act of violence against your spouse or your child, you shouldn't have a gun."

———

Columbus Police Academy, Columbus, Ohio, August 26, 1996:

"Now, again, there are people who are against banning cop-killer bullets. They say it's just a slippery slope eroding their right to keep and bear arms. I have never seen a deer in a Kevlar vest. Never. If somebody can show me a picture of one out there hiding from our hunters, I'll be glad to reassess my position. But until they do I believe I'll stay with these folks here; I think they're entitled to be safe."

———

LINE ITEM VETO

"For years, presidents of both parties have pounded this very desk in frustration at having to sign necessary legislation that contained special-interest boondoggles, tax loopholes, and pure pork. The line item veto will give us a chance to change that, to permit presidents to better represent the public interest by cutting waste, protecting taxpayers, and balancing the budget."

———

Signing of Line Item Veto Bill, April 9, 1997:

"Let me say in closing before I sign the bill that it is customary for a president to give the pens he uses to sign a bill into law to those who did the most for its passage. So I am honored today to send the very first four pens that are used here to the former presidents who also made the line item veto their cause—President Reagan and President Ford, President Carter, President Bush. I thank them and our country thanks them. Their successors will be able to use this power that they long sought to eliminate waste from the federal budget, to advance our values, and protect our priorities as we move into the twenty-first century."

———

MEDICARE

"I believe we have a duty to care for our parents so that they can live their lives in dignity. That duty includes securing Medicare, slowing the rate of growth of inflation, protecting our senior citizens, and giving them every opportunity to maximize the options that are out there.''

———

"You know, Medicare has the lowest administrative cost of any health-insurance plan in America, private or public. It has done a basically good job. There are more seniors now on the plan than ever before. We have to deal with the population problems that exist now and the ones that are going to exist in the future.

"But we have the ability right now to put ten years into the life of the Medicare trust fund, and we ought to just do it. We ought to just go on and do that. We can do that with no problem, and we can do it in the context of a balanced-budget plan.''

———

"American seniors have the highest life expectancy in the world. We need to reform it, not wreck it.''

———

THE MILITARY

State of the Union Address, January 25, 1994:

"But nothing, nothing is more important to our security than our nation's armed forces. We honor their contributions, including those who are carrying out the longest humanitarian airlift in history in Bosnia; those who will complete their mission in Somalia this year, and their brave comrades who gave their lives there.

"Our forces are the finest military our nation has ever had. And I have pledged that as long as I am president, they will remain the best-equipped, the best-trained, and the best-prepared fighting force on the face of the Earth.''

On his lack of military service during Vietnam:

"One of the few tangible memories I have of my father is a picture of him in uniform. I grew up believing in the honor of the military. It *killed* me to turn against the war."

———

December 5, 1996:

"Today our brave men and women in uniform are helping other people in other lands to make their peace. And across our country this holiday season people are joining in peace to feed the hungry, to bring toys to poor children who otherwise would not have them and to reconcile our own differences."

———

NUCLEAR WEAPONS

Speech to the United Nations, October 1993:

"If we do not stem the proliferation of the world's deadliest weapons, no democracy can feel secure."

———

"I will also tell you when you hear a word like *nuclear proliferation,* it may sound like a big old word and you can't imagine what it means. It means, among other things, that tonight and in the last two years for the first time since the dawn of the nuclear age, there is not a single nuclear weapon pointed at the children of the United States."

Peace

December 6, 1995:

"Let us resolve, my fellow Americans, to be peacemakers. For just as so many nations around the world and so many children around the world cry for peace, so do we need peace here at home in our toughest neighborhoods, where there are children, so many children who deserve to have their childhood and their future free and peaceful."

———

"As we look around the world tonight we know the spirit of peace is strong enough to triumph over the forces that still threaten it. Let us be grateful that our nation is at peace and rejoice in the progress we have made to bring about peace on Earth. And let us not forget the work still to be done, from Bosnia to the Middle East to the Korean Peninsula."

———

Race

1992:

"The American people are so much more alike at a human level than they think they are, from how much they love their kids to how badly they want to be safe, how concerned they are about their jobs and their futures. I'd like to be remembered for making people really believe that we're all better off when we define our lives in terms of our common purposes, for really helping to reestablish a sense of community and bridging the troubled waters of race—particularly race—and all the other things dividing this country. I think life is lonelier than it ought to be in America because we are so isolated from one another."

Speaking on the steps of the Arkansas Old State House, the site of two conventions in 1861 which led to the state's secession from the Union just before the Civil War:

"For twelve years, the Republicans have tried to divide us, race against race. Here in the shadow of this great building, all of us know all about race-baiting. They've used that old tool on us for decades now. And I want to tell you one thing: I understand that tactic, and I will not let them get away with it in 1992."

"Because of my background, because I'm a Southerner, because I've had a real commitment to healing between the races and because of my own civil-rights record, I might be in a position to do that in a way that others haven't."

RESEARCH

"Every time we send a mission into space we learn something else about how the human body works and we learn something else about the earth's environment that will help our children and our grandchildren create opportunity and live in a better world. The investments we have made in the last few years have reaped untold benefits. The average life expectancy of people with AIDS and HIV has more than doubled in the last four years alone because of medical research and moving drugs to market faster."

"We must free science and medicine from the grasp of politics."

———

"One of the marvelous things we have learned about research is that it's not necessarily going to benefit just a particular category in which it was undertaken, that ideas don't stay in boxes anymore, that they all become more interrelated, the more you know and the more you learn."

———

RIGHTS

"Now that we don't have to worry about Moscow we can finally give content to our saying that human rights is central. We can help in all kinds of humanitarian ways where we couldn't before because we feared war with the Soviets."

———

"I don't think we have to choose between increasing trade and fostering human rights and open societies."

———

State of the Union Address, January 25, 1994:

"As we expand opportunity, no one can be left out. We must continue to enforce fair lending and fair housing, and all civil-rights laws, because America will never be complete in its renewal until everyone shares in its bounty."

———

November 1995:

"The battle for civil rights was fought in our courts, our government, our communities and our homes, but the greatest victories took place in the hearts and minds of Americans."

TAXES

1991:

"In a Clinton administration, we are going to have a national strategy to compete in the world and put Americans back to work. We need to give people incentives to make a long-term investment in America and reward people who produce goods and services, not those who speculate with other people's money. We've got to invest more money in emerging technologies to help keep high-paying jobs here at home. We've got to convert from a defense to a domestic economy. For twelve years the Republicans have raised taxes on the middle class. I believe it's time to give the middle class tax relief."

1992 campaign:

"I don't blame Senator Tsongas. He would rather beat on the middle-class tax cuts because we know all the upscale people who write editorials think it is frivolous. It is not, and I will say again, we are waging class warfare. I think a great country can afford to be more just. Let's quit making these political speeches and talk about how you are going to change people's lives."

TECHNOLOGY

"When I became president, I was amazed at just the way the White House worked . . . in outmoded ways that didn't take maximum advantage of technology and didn't do things that any business would have done years ago."

———

"I don't have a computer in the Oval Office, but we have quite a nice one over in the residence. When I'm at home—thanks largely to Chelsea, who's taught me most of what I know about computers—we've had a lot of fun with it, playing all those complex games I can't begin to do as well as she does."

———

"A hundred years ago we moved from farm to factory. Now we move to an age of technology, information, and global competition. These changes have opened vast new opportunities for our people, but they have also presented them with stiff challenges. While more Americans are living better, too many of our fellow citizens are working harder just to keep up, and they are rightly concerned about the security of their families."

———

"The great computer genius who is the head of Microsoft, Bill Gates, says that the transformation in technology we're undergoing in communications is the greatest in five hundred years; that the digital chip is the most significant thing to happen in the way people communicate with each other since Gutenberg printed the first Bible in Europe five hundred years ago."

———

"Every citizen can now read the *Congressional Record*. If you have insomnia, I recommend it. Every citizen can get the text of what's in a new law the very day it passes. Art lovers can go to the Louvre. Baseball fans can pay an on-line visit to Cooperstown. Everyone can find a passage in the Bible or in Shakespeare with the click of a mouse. Most of all the Internet will be the most profoundly revolutionary tool for educating our children in generations."

———

WELFARE

"We will scrap the current welfare system and make welfare a second chance, not a way of life. We will empower people on welfare with the education, training, and child care they need for up to two years so they can break the cycle of dependency. After that, those who can work will have to go to work, either by taking a job in the private sector or through community service."

———

October 1992:

"I think that upper-middle-class people are ready to be challenged to help people in the cities help themselves. That's why welfare reform has such a powerful resonance in the suburbs. It is not because people want to punish poor people. It's because the experience of people living in the suburbs is that they helped themselves into the suburbs. You speak to the suburbs not maintaining dependence but creating independence. I think that has a powerful resonance, because it makes what you want to do with poor folks consistent with the life experience of middle- and upper-middle-class America."

———

1993—*Threatening to veto the welfare-reform bill if it emerges in a form he doesn't like:*

"You can put wings on a pig, but you don't make it an eagle."

———

"Most Americans believe that working, even if it's in a subsidized job, is preferable to just drawing welfare and not working. I made that clear all along, that if we're going to end welfare after a two-year period, people had to be able to work. And if there was not work in the private sector, then we'd have to create the jobs. Second, I think that this bill, plus the earned-income tax credit, plus providing health-care coverage to people in low-wage jobs, will dramatically undermine the whole basis of dependency. Finally, we go after what is the real source of this problem, which is the inordinate number of out-of-wedlock births in this country. I think all these things put together give us a real chance to end welfare as we know it."

———

State of the Union Address, January 24, 1995:

"Nothing has done more to undermine our sense of common responsibility than our failed welfare system. It rewards welfare over work. It undermines family values."

———

"And think how we'll feel if there's no politics in poverty. Think how we'll feel if we know that we treat everybody the same. And sure, at any given time in our country's life, there will always be some people out of work. But there won't be this separate class of people who literally we have isolated and hurt terribly by not imposing more responsibility and giving more opportunity to, and their kids."

WOMEN

"Throughout our history, American women have done what they had to do, and that was quite a lot. They fought for the right to vote, they kept America afloat in wartime, they raised and nurtured families, and they added careers to raising families."

———

"I am the son of a remarkable woman, the husband of an extraordinary woman, and the proud father of a very special young woman. Each has shaped my life in wonderful ways."

———

Ypsilanti, Michigan, October 30, 1996:

"Women are establishing businesses and creating new jobs at twice the national rate of business and job growth. One-third of all the businesses in our country, about eight million companies now, are owned by women. They employ one in five of American workers."

———

Human Rights Day, December 10, 1996:

"We cannot advance our ideals and interests unless we focus more attention on the fundamental human rights and basic needs of women and girls. We must recognize that it is a violation of human rights when girls and women are sold into prostitution, when rape becomes a weapon of war, when women are denied the right to plan their own families, including through forced abortions, when young girls are brutalized by genital mutilation, when women around the world are unsafe even in their own homes. If women are free from violence, if they're healthy and educated, if they can live and work as full and equal partners in any society, then families will flourish. And when they do, communities and nations will thrive."

Looking to
the Future

"We Americans are a people both privileged and challenged. We were formed in turbulent times, and we stand now at the beginning of a new time, the dawn of a new era. Our deeds and decisions can lift America up so that in our third century we will continue to be the youngest and most optimistic of nations; of people on the march once again, strong and unafraid. If we are bold in our hopes, if we meet our great responsibilities, we will give the country we love the best years it has ever known."

———

July 19, 1995:

"President Lincoln said, we cannot escape our history. We cannot escape our future, either. And that future must be one in which every American has the chance to live up to his or her God-given capacities."

July 2, 1996:

"I believe with all my heart that the best days of this country are still ahead of us. And when I imagine what I want America to look like when my daughter is my age and, hopefully, I've got a whole nest of grandkids to worry about, when I've long since forgotten about politics, I want it to be the most peaceful period in world history. I want it to be a period where people compete with one another in economics, education and athletics, and not in military contests."

———

Eighty-seventh Annual Convention of the NAACP, July 10, 1996:
"We can't remake our yesterdays, we can only make tomorrows."

Asked about what happens after his two terms, when he will be fifty-four:

"I will try not to get in my successor's hair. I will try to take a little more time for personal things. And I will try to spend a lot of time doing whatever Hillary wants to do. I am not worried about it. I will find something useful to do."

BRIDGE BUILDING

Democratic National Convention, Chicago, Illinois, August 29, 1996:

"Our bridge to the future must include bridges to other nations, because we remain the world's indispensable nation to advance prosperity, peace and freedom, and to keep our own children safe from the dangers of terror and weapons of mass destruction."

1996 campaign:

"Now, here's the main idea. I love and revere the rich and proud history of America. And I am determined to take our best traditions into the future. But with all respect, we do not need to build a bridge to the past."

From Little Rock victory speech:

"We've got a bridge to build, and I'm ready if you are."

September 7, 1996:

"And what we have to do is, as I have said until I'm blue in the face, build a bridge to the future that gives opportunity to everybody, expects responsibility from everybody, and then says, if you are willing to share our values and play by the rules, we don't care anything else about you. You don't have to tell us anything else. We don't care about what your race is, whether you're a man or woman, whether you're old or young, whether you've got a disability. We don't care. If you're willing to do your best and be a part of this, our bridge is going to be big enough for you to go across, because we'll all be better off if you're better off. And we're going to have an American community. And my wife is right: It does take a village. And we are going to do it together."

ON TO THE TWENTY-FIRST CENTURY

To Foreign Policy Association, New York, New York, April 1, 1992:

"In 1992, we must look forward, not backward. I seek not to be the last president of the twentieth century, but the first president for the twenty-first century."

First Inaugural Address, January 20, 1993:

"And so my fellow Americans, as we stand at the edge of the twenty-first century, let us begin with energy and hope, with faith and discipline, and let us work until our work is done. The scripture says, 'And let us not be weary in well-doing, for in due season, we shall reap, if we faint not.' "

"Our country is changing just as profoundly as it did when we moved from farm to factory, from the country to the cities and towns a hundred years ago. The microchip and the global marketplace are opening up undreamed-of prospects, but real challenges. If we want to keep the American dream alive for every single person who is willing to work for it, we know that more than ever before, we have to give all Americans the skills, the education they need to be winners in this time of change. We must not send our children into a twenty-first century unprepared for the world they will inhabit and the jobs they will have to fill.

"The twenty-first century is America's for the taking—if we are bold enough and strong enough and confident enough to go forward together. We will make the best of this new technology together. We will educate our children with it, improve our businesses with it, make our government more democratic with it, and build a brighter, freer, more prosperous future with it. That is the American way. Let the future begin."